FAST ACCURATE BIDS

Apparel Decorating Estimating Software

User's Manual

Version 3.5

Contents

Introduction

Fast Accurate Bids takes the guesswork and drudgery out of the bid generation process. This easy-to-use Windows software provides one-page convenience for configuring item decorations, efficiency in looking up items, and an automated link to Microsoft Word for printing out the finished bid.

The figures below give an overview of how the software is organized.

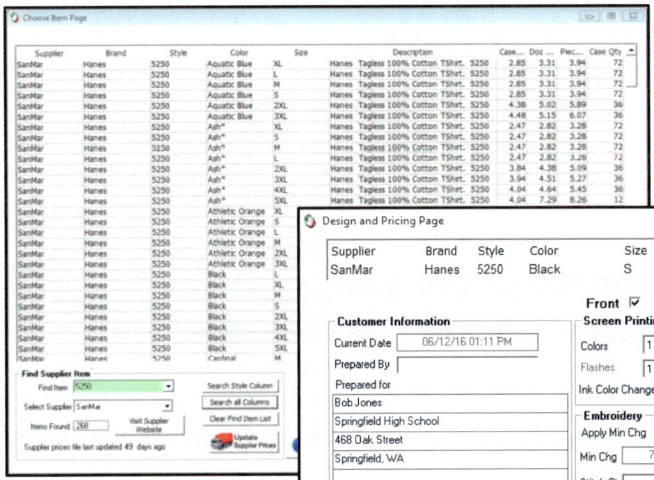

The Choose Item Page provides quick access to items and can be easily updated to ensure pricing accuracy.

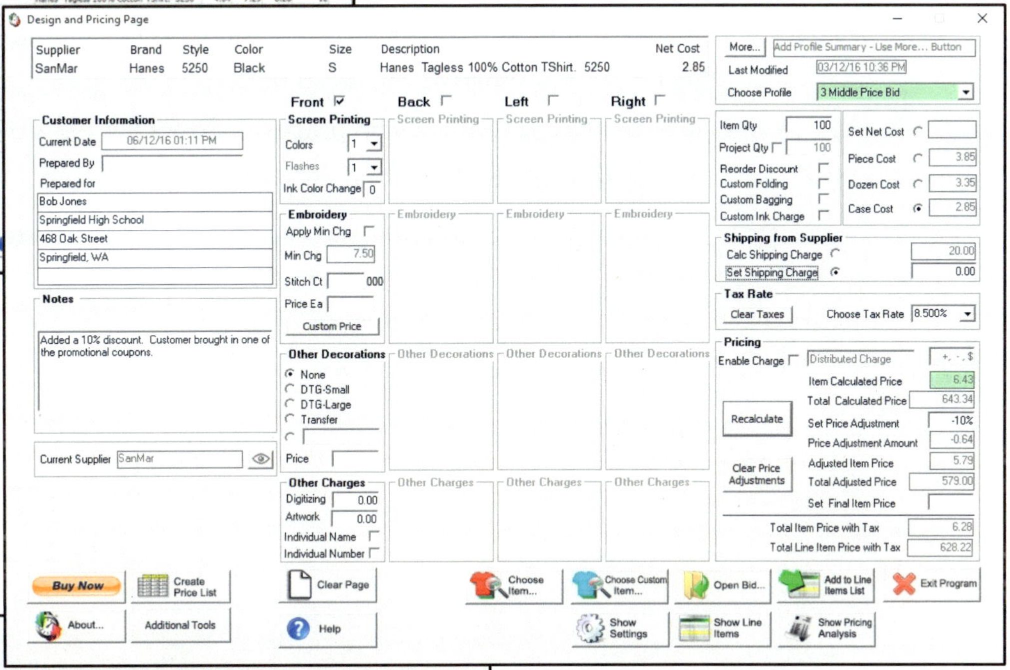

The Design and Pricing Page provides simplicity in selecting decoration tasks and pricing.

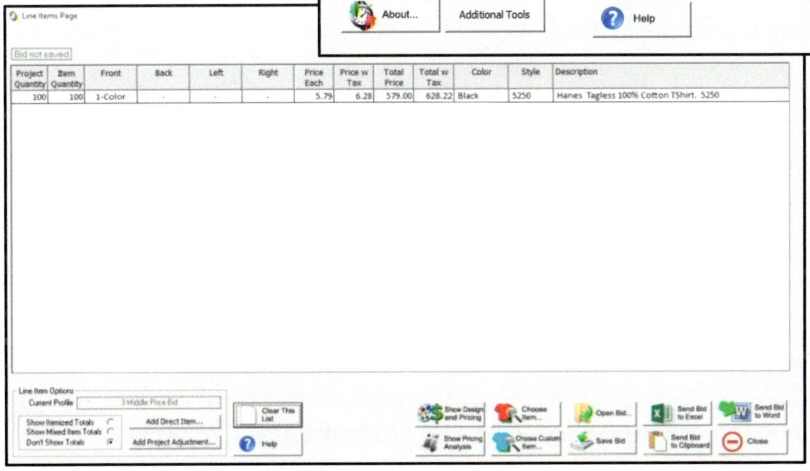

The Line Items Page keeps track of the line item data automatically as you build the bid.

With a single click, you can copy the line items list to the Windows clipboard to paste into an email, save it to Microsoft Excel, or save it to the Microsoft Word custom bids file that comes with Fast Accurate Bids.

Tools for Learning Fast Accurate Bids

Fast Accurate Bids provides a document called **Sample Bids.pdf** that you can find in the directory **My Documents | Fast Accurate Bids | Documents** on the computer on which you installed the software.[1]

The Sample Bids document provides some typical bids and typical change requests that customers might ask for. In coordination with this document, you can access each of the sample bids from within the Fast Accurate Bids software by clicking the Open Bid button on either the Design and Pricing Page or the Line Items Page. You can also watch videos on how each of the bids and change requests was done by going to www.FastAccurateBids.com/Videos .

Consider using the Sample Bids document, sample bids, and the associated videos as a self-paced course for learning how to use the software. We suggest:

1. Start by reading the description of the Standard Bid in the Sample Bids document.
2. Open the Standard Bid from within Fast Accurate Bids to see how to open a bid and what the Line Items Page for a finished bid looks like.
3. Watch the video to see the step-by-step process of how the bid was created.
4. Use Fast Accurate Bids to create the bid on your own.
5. Work your way through all of the sample bids and suggested changes to the sample bids.

[1] The **My Documents** directory is the same directory as **Library | Documents,** whichever computer file path you are accustomed to using will bring you to the same files.

Types of bids you can create

Fast Accurate Bids lets you create any type of bid that you want. You have control over setting up the line items in the way that you feel best communicates your pricing to your customers and you can edit the Word file that provides the explanation of the bid to provide whatever additional information that you want.

The sections that follow describe the three most common types of apparel decoration bids.

Standard Bids

Standard bids present an assortment of choices so the customer can choose one. For example, a standard bid might offer a choice of quantities (24, 36, 48), or a choice of garments (good, better, best) to allow the customer to select the one that is the best match for he wants. Standard bids show the price per item and don't provide a totals row since the underlying assumption is that the customer will only select one of the options offered by the bid.

Here's the line items list for the Fast Accurate Bids sample standard bid.

Line Items Page

Sample Bid - Standard Bid on T-Shirts in a Selection of Quantities and Decorations.bid

Project Quantity	Item Quantity	Front	Back	Left	Right	Price Each	Price w Tax	Total Price	Total w Tax	Color	Style	Description
24	24	3-Color	-	-	-	12.38	13.12	297.12	314.95	Black	2000	Gildan Ultra Cotton 100% Cotton TShirt. 2000
36	36	3-Color	-	-	-	9.91	10.50	356.76	378.17	Black	2000	Gildan Ultra Cotton 100% Cotton TShirt. 2000
48	48	3-Color	-	-	-	9.06	9.60	434.88	460.97	Black	2000	Gildan Ultra Cotton 100% Cotton TShirt. 2000
24	24	3-Color	1-Color	-	-	15.31	16.23	367.44	389.49	Black	2000	Gildan Ultra Cotton 100% Cotton TShirt. 2000
36	36	3-Color	1-Color	-	-	12.00	12.72	432.00	457.92	Black	2000	Gildan Ultra Cotton 100% Cotton TShirt. 2000
48	48	3-Color	1-Color	-	-	10.98	11.64	527.04	558.66	Black	2000	Gildan Ultra Cotton 100% Cotton TShirt. 2000
24	24	3-Color	2-Color	-	-	17.14	18.17	411.36	436.04	Black	2000	Gildan Ultra Cotton 100% Cotton TShirt. 2000
36	36	3-Color	2-Color	-	-	13.18	13.97	474.48	502.95	Black	2000	Gildan Ultra Cotton 100% Cotton TShirt. 2000
48	48	3-Color	2-Color	-	-	11.98	12.70	575.04	609.54	Black	2000	Gildan Ultra Cotton 100% Cotton TShirt. 2000

Mixed Item Bids

Mixed item bids present an assortment of items that will receive the same decoration. For example, a mixed item bid might offer the pricing for placing the same image on 100 T-Shirts, 25 sweatshirts, and 25 hoodies. Mixed item bids show the price per item and can optionally have a totals row as well to show the total number of items and the total price for the job.

Here's the line items list for the Fast Accurate Bids sample mixed item bid.

Line Items Page

Sample Bid - Mixed Item Bid on T-Shirts and Hoodies.bid

Project Quantity	Item Quantity	Front	Back	Left	Right	Price Each	Price w Tax	Total Price	Total w Tax	Color	Style	Description
100	60	3-Color	2-Color	-	-	10.24	10.85	614.40	651.26	Black	2000	Gildan Ultra Cotton 100% Cotton TShirt. 2000
100	12	3-Color	2-Color	-	-	12.79	13.56	153.48	162.69	Black	2000	XXL Gildan Ultra Cotton 100% Cotton TShirt. 2000
100	6	3-Color	2-Color	-	-	13.36	14.16	80.16	84.97	Black	2000	XXXL Gildan Ultra Cotton 100% Cotton TShirt. 2000
100	12	3-Color	2-Color	-	-	23.05	24.43	276.60	293.20	Black	18500	Gildan Heavy Blend Hooded Sweatshirt. 18500
100	6	3-Color	2-Color	-	-	26.07	27.63	156.42	165.81	Black	18500	XXL Gildan Heavy Blend Hooded Sweatshirt. 18500
100	4	3-Color	2-Color	-	-	26.62	28.22	106.48	112.87	Black	18500	XXXL Gildan Heavy Blend Hooded Sweatshirt. 18500
	100							1,387.54	1,470.80			

Use the field Project Quantity on the Design and Pricing Page when doing mixed item screen printing bids to prevent redundant screen charges.

Itemized Bids

Itemized bids show the pricing for each of the components of an apparel decoration job as opposed to standard bids and mixed item bids which show inclusive pricing. For example, an itemized bid for embroidery might show the price for the undecorated garment, the digitizing, and the embroidery. Itemized bids often show both a total price per item and total price for the job.

Here's the line items list for the Fast Accurate Bids sample itemized bid for embroidery.

Line Items Page

Sample Bid - Itemized Bid with Embroidery Pricing for Jackets, Embroidery, and Digitizing.bid

Project Quantity	Item Quantity	Front	Back	Left	Right	Price Each	Price w Tax	Total Price	Total w Tax	Color	Style	Description
24	24	-	-	-	-	52.81	55.98	1,267.44	1,343.49	Chestnut ...	J754	Port Authority Challenger Jacket. J754
24	1	-	-	-	-	0.83	0.88	20.00	21.20	-	-	Digitizing Front Design $20
24	24	Emb	-	-	-	7.50	7.95	180.00	190.80	-	-	Front Embroidery Only
24	1	-	-	-	-	1.67	1.77	40.00	42.40	-	-	Digitizing Back Design $40
24	24	-	Emb	-	-	22.50	23.85	540.00	572.40	-	-	Back Embroidery Only
24	24	-	-	-	-	0.50	0.53	12.00	12.72	-	-	Poly Bagging
						85.81	90.96	2,059.44	2,183.01			

When creating itemized bids for screen printing, if you intend to itemize the cost of preparing the screens, be sure to set up set up a pricing profile for the screens and a pricing profile for the shirts and decorations. The pricing profile for the shirts and decorations should have the field **Screen Charge per Color** set to $0.00. For more information, see the Fast Accurate Bids Shop Owner's Manual.

Steps for creating a standard bid

Fast Accurate Bids automates the bid creation process with point-and-click convenience. The Quick Start Guide shown below provides a general overview of the steps involved in creating bids.

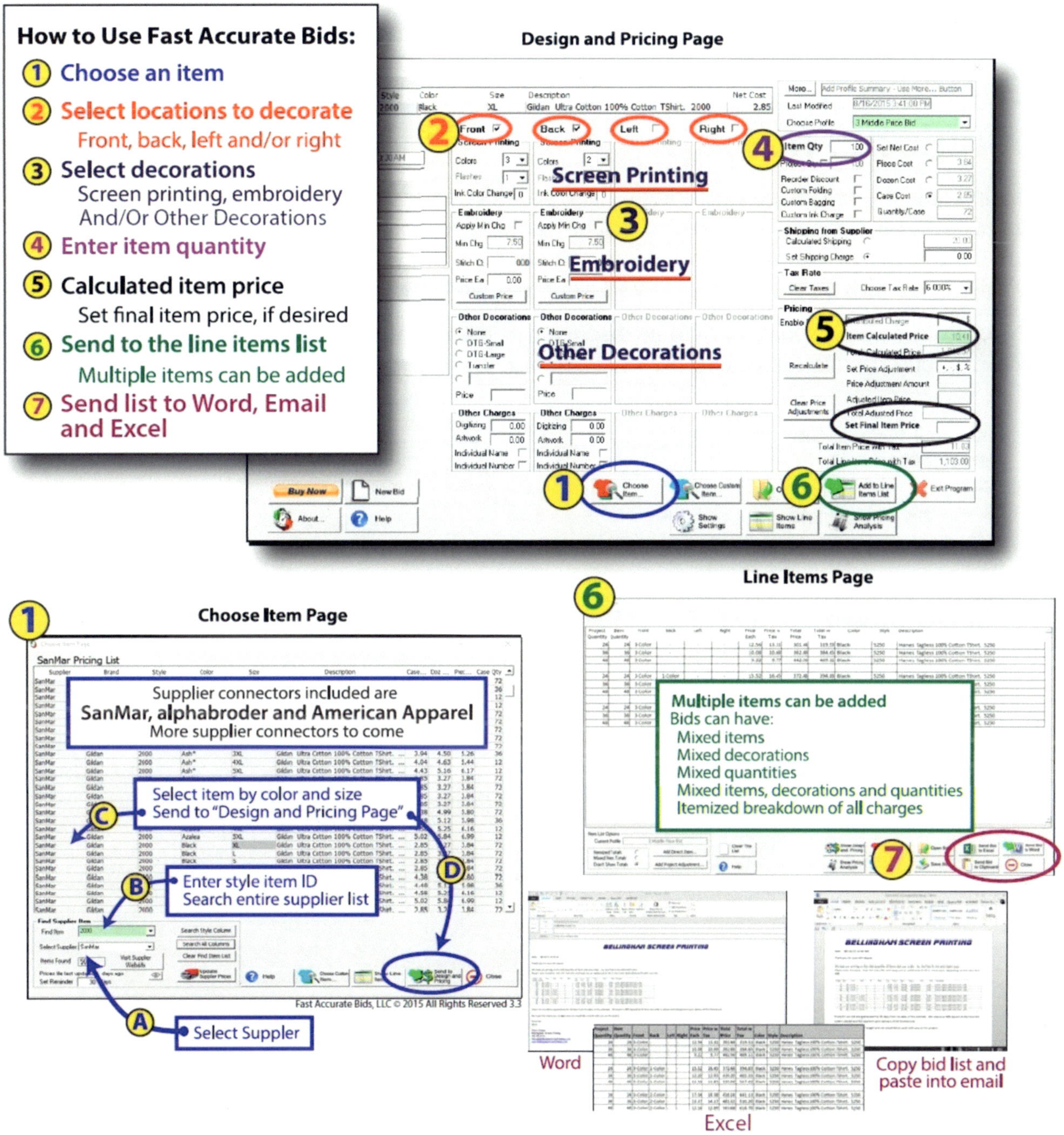

There are many additional features in Fast Accurate Bids, which are described in this manual and in the *Fast Accurate Bids Shop Owner's Manual*. Consider using the Quick Start Guide as a handy roadmap while you are still learning how to use Fast Accurate Bids.

This manual provides step-by-step instructions on how to create bids generally and how to use the features of Fast Accurate Bids that relate to bid creation.

For example, let's suppose you want to create a bid for quantities of 50, 100 and 150 black shirts with a 1-color screen print on the front, and you give the customer a 10% discount. The next several sections describe the steps for how to create a bid using these specifications.

Entering customer information and additional notes

The left side of the Design and Pricing Page provides an area in which to enter the sales person's name, customer's name and address, and any notes you want to add for the current line item. You only need to enter the customer information once and can do so at any time before finalizing the bid. It remains on screen in case you want to update it or add additional information.

The customer name you enter will be displayed at the top of the Line Items page, and automatically carried forward to the finalized bid.

1. Enter your name as the person preparing the bid.
2. Click in the first line and enter the customer's name.
3. Press the Tab key or click on subsequent lines to enter the rest of the contact information.
4. Click in the Notes box and enter whatever notes you want.

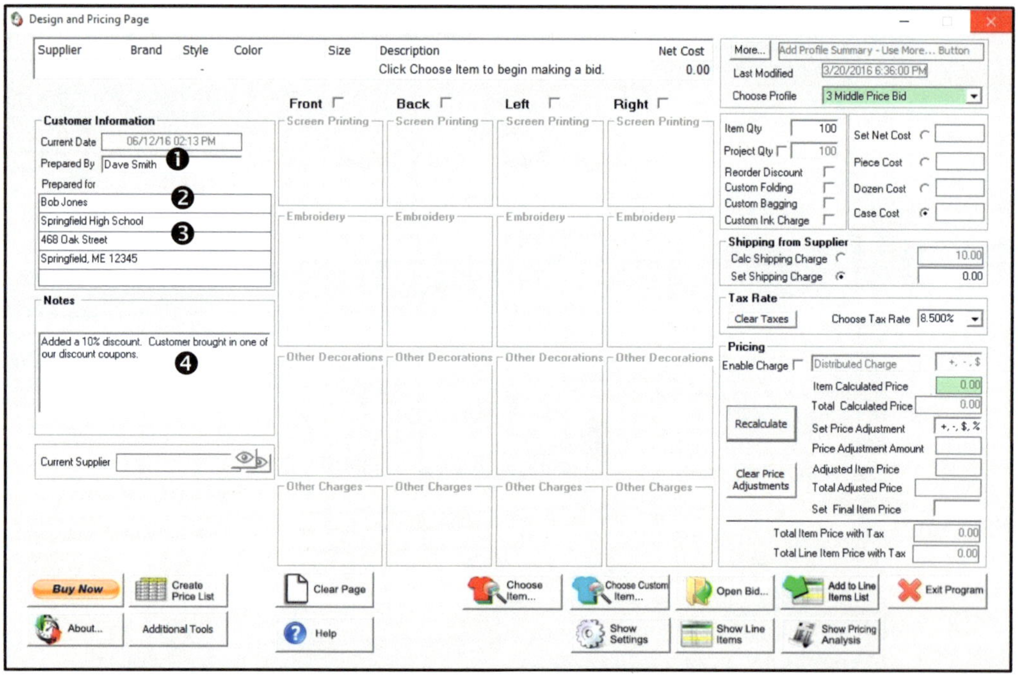

To move from line to line in the **Prepared For** entry box, press the Tab key or click on each new line.

Things to note

- The **Current Date** is a display field that makes a record of the date and time the current line item is entered. This field cannot be edited.
- Any notes you enter will be associated with the current line item. Once created, they can be viewed from the Design and Pricing Page or the Pricing Analysis Page. The notes do not get carried forward to the finished bid. They are for your reference only.
- The Pricing Analysis Page is a separate page in Fast Accurate Bids. It provides detailed data on the pricing for the current line item. Select the **Show on Pricing Analysis** check box to include the customer information at the top of the Pricing Analysis Page.
- If you do not see the check box for **Show on Pricing Analysis**, it means that your shop owner has set up a password for Fast Accurate Bids and you are using the program in user mode.
- The fields and check boxes for specifying the decoration tasks are organized by area of the item. The check box at the top of each area (**Front**, **Back**, **Left**, and **Right**) allows you to activate it. Unless the activation check box has been selected, the area for the decoration choices will be blank.

Selecting the pricing profile

An important thing to understand when using Fast Accurate Bids is that different pricing profiles will result in different bid amounts for the same items with the same decoration tasks. Make sure you choose the pricing profile that is the correct choice for the bid you want to produce.

1. Click the down arrow and select the pricing profile.
   E.g., select 3 **Middle Price Bid**.

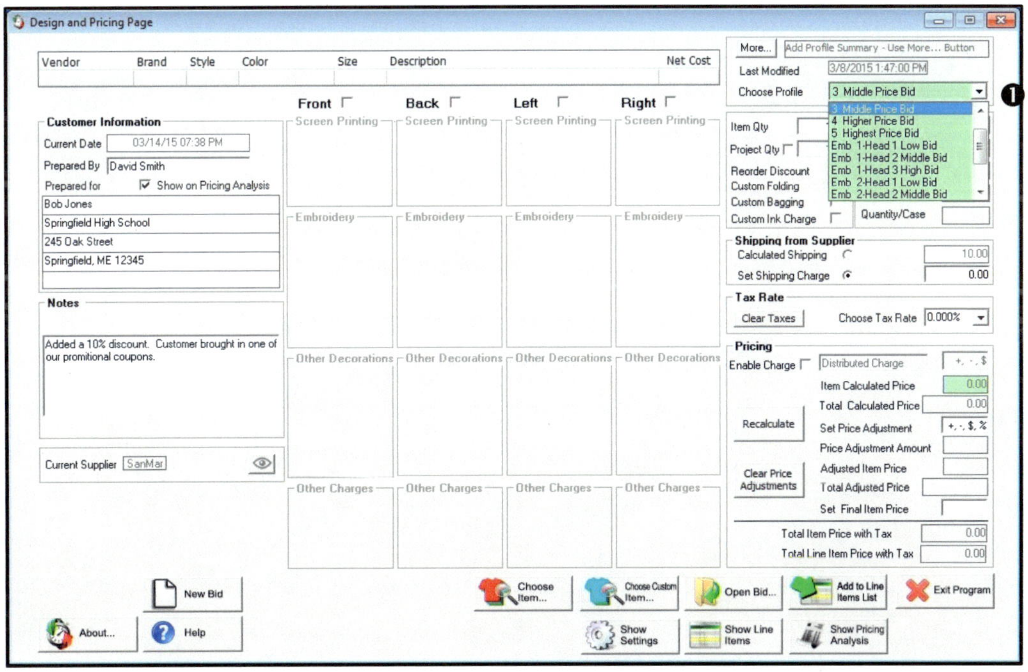

Things to note

- Fast Accurate Bids comes with several built-in pricing profiles. Each pricing profile is a set of charges, markups, and other variable settings for the program. For example, three of the pricing profiles that come with the software are **1 Lowest Price Bid**, **3 Middle Price Bid**, and **5 Highest Price Bid**. These are intended for use for screen printing bids.

- The built-in pricing profiles are read-only files but the can be used as the starting point for creating custom pricing profiles for your business so that the bids you create accurately reflect your current pricing. This means that your bids will be accurate, consistent, and repeatable.
- You can also create additional pricing profiles. For example, you may wish to add a pricing profile for bids for nonprofit organizations.
- If you're new to the screen printing business, you can start immediately by using the **3 Middle Price Bid** pricing profile for most jobs, the **2 Lower Price Bid** pricing profile for highly competitive bids, and the **4 Higher Price Bid** pricing profile when working on jobs for customers who are willing to pay more to get exactly what they need.
- If you're an embroiderer, you can start by using the built-in profiles for embroidery. Select the one that's appropriate for your equipment. For example, if you have a 1-head machine, start with **Emb 1-Head 1 Middle Bid**.
- If you're a seasoned business owner, you can easily edit the pricing profiles to generate precisely the bid pricing you want. You may also create as many additional pricing profiles as you want. For example, if you work with governmental agencies, you may wish to set up a specific pricing profile for those jobs.
- The *Fast Accurate Bids Shop Owner's Manual* provides in-depth information on how to edit and create additional pricing profiles.

Specifying the quantity and selecting the decoration tasks

The Design and Pricing Page allows rapid entry of the decoration tasks and pricing you want associated with a line item. Begin by specifying the quantity for the line item and selecting the decoration tasks. Fast Accurate Bids provides two fields for quantity. **Item Qty** is for the quantity for this particular line item. **Project Qty** is for screen printing mixed item bids. If the customer wants the same decoration on different types of items, select the check box for **Project Qty** and enter the total quantity of items for the bid in the **Project Quantity** field.

The fields and check boxes for specifying the decoration tasks are organized by area of the item. The check box at the top of each area allows you to activate it. Unless the activation check box has been selected, the area for the decoration choices will be blank.

1. Enter the item quantity for the first line item (e.g., 50).
2. Click the check box for Front to activate that area of the item.
3. Select the number of screen print colors for the front (e.g., 1).
4. Select the number of flashes for the front (e.g., 1.)
5. Click Choose Item to open the Choose Item Page.

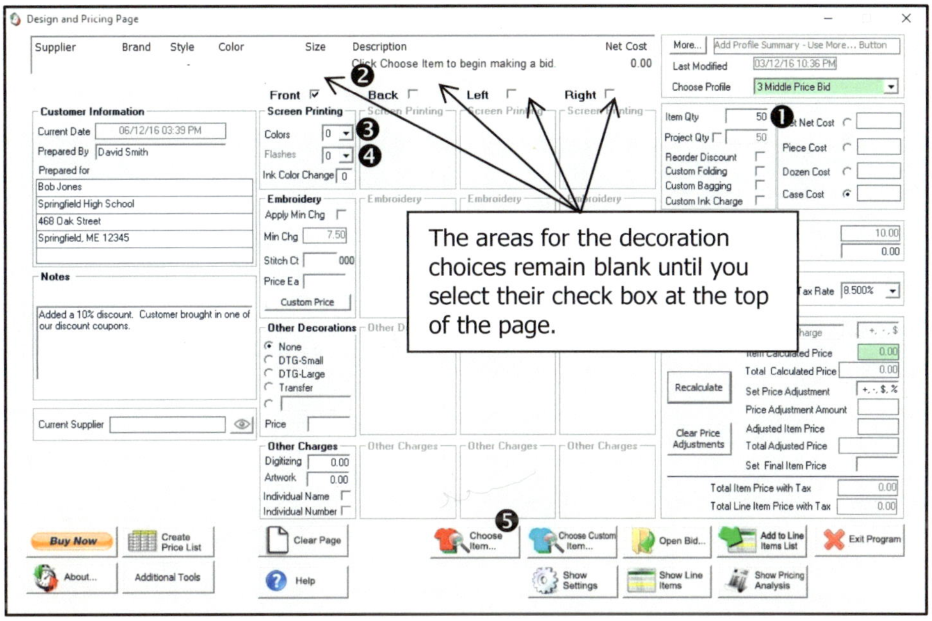

Things to note

- The quantity pricing breaks on item markup, screen printing discounts, embroidery discounts, and other decoration discounts are taken from tables on the currently selected Fast Accurate Bids pricing profile.
- To view the settings for the pricing profile, click the **Show Settings** button at the bottom of the Design and Pricing Page. If you do not see this button, it means that your shop owner has set up a password for Fast Accurate Bids and you are using the program in user mode.
- The *Fast Accurate Bids Shop Owner's Manual* documents the pricing profiles and how to use the Profile Settings Page to configure them for your business. It also provides information on setting a password for Fast Accurate Bids and the difference between User Mode and Owner Mode when using the software.

- The combination of the **Item Qty** and the **Project Qty** fields allows you to automatically calculate the best possible pricing for your customers when you are screen printing the same image on a mix of items such as T-shirts, hoodies, jackets, etc. Use the **Item Qty** field for the quantity for the current line item. Use the **Project Qty** field for total number of items to be printed with the same image.
- If you do not see the decoration choices, select the check box for the area (**Front**, **Back**, **Left**, **and Right**) to reveal the choices for the decoration.

Selecting an item from the Choose Item Page

Clicking the **Choose Item** button on the Design and Pricing Page opens the Choose Item Page. To begin the item selection process, make sure the field **Select Supplier** displays the correct supplier for the item you want, enter a search string for the item you want in the field **Find Item**, and then click one of the two **Search** buttons. This brings information from the supplier's pricing file into the Choose Item Page. Select the item you want, and click the **Send to Design and Pricing** button.

1. Select the supplier you want to use. For example, select **SanMar**.
2. Enter a search term for looking up the item. For example, enter **5250**.
3. Click one of the two **Search** buttons.
4. Select the item from the list.
5. Click **Send to Design and Pricing**.
   Tip: Double-clicking on an item also sends it to the Design and Pricing Page.

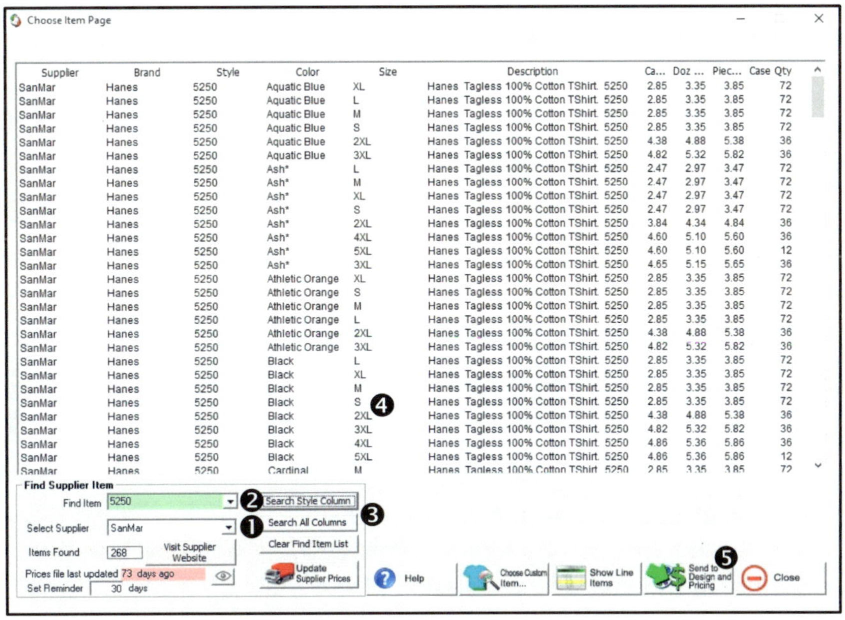

Things to Note

- When looking up items by clicking the **Search Style Column** button, Fast Accurate Bids displays only the results for the specific style in the Find Item field in the list on the Choose Item Page.
- To bring the supplier's full pricing file in the Choose Item Page, enter the search term **ALL** in the Find Item field and then click **Search Style Column**. (Using ALL works for all the suppliers except SanMar.)
- Looking up items by clicking the **Search All Columns** button displays all the items in the supplier's price file that contain the search string in the columns **Description**, **Color**, **Size**, or **Style**. For example, if you search SanMar for Tshirt, you will see results for all the SanMar Tshirts but also all the Sweatshirts because the word **Sweatshirts** contains the string **tshirts** within it.
- The number of items returned by a search may appear overwhelming at first. Just choose a representative size and color for the line item for your bid. For example, if the customer wants a bid on white 5250 T-shirts in an assortment of sizes, select a white 5250 for any of the regular sizes.

- Fast Accurate Bids does not carry forward the item size to the Line Items List. When doing a bid that requires specifying quantities by size, edit the item description for each of the line items to add the size to the item description.
- If you want to see the images for items, click **Visit Supplier Website**. This will open your supplier's website to give you access to search for the style you want. When you find the item you want, copy and paste its style ID into the **Find Item** field and click the Search button.
- If the supplier doesn't offer the item you want, click **Add Custom Item** and enter the item information in Custom Item Page that appears.
- Because the pricing for items changes frequently, it's important that the Fast Accurate Bids Choose Item Page has access to the current pricing for your suppliers. Fast Accurate Bids provides supplier connector software for updating pricing.
- For information on how to update the item pricing see the section of the *Fast Accurate Bids Shop Owner's Manual* called "Updating supplier pricing files."
- The field at the lower left of the Choose Item Page displays how long it's been since the supplier's pricing file was last updated. It is up to you to update the data on the Choose Item Page to keep your pricing current.
- If there is pink highlighting on the number of days since the supplier pricing file was last updated, it means that the number of days since the pricing file was last updated is greater than the number of days specified in the field **Set Reminder**, which appears just below it.
- If you anticipate that the customer needs items in sizes XXL and larger, the bid information for these items can by handled by adding a separate line item for the larger sizes or by adding a note to the text of the finished bid to indicate the additional amount for larger sizes.
- If you notice that an item is not available from the Choose Item Page, it may be because (1) you have not selected the correct supplier for the item; (2) the item is new and you need to update the supplier's pricing file to have access to it or; (3) the item is one that the supplier represents and takes the orders for on their website, but they have not included it in their downloadable pricing file. For example, alphabroder does not include pricing in their downloadable pricing file for items they offer which are actually manufactured and sold by another company. In other words, the selected supplier does not stock the item, it only takes the orders and the other company controls the pricing and order fulfillment. Typically, you will see the term "drop ship" either near or as part of the item ID for these items. Drop shipped means that the supplier takes the orders and has the other company ship them to you. For example, alphabroder does not stock the **Dickies Drop Ship; DCP118 Long-Sleeve 8-Button Chef Coat** and, for this reason, the alphabroder price list does not have this item.
- Alphabroder recommends contacting your alphabroder sales representative for a fuller understanding of why items listed on their website may be missing from the downloadable pricing file that is available to you. According to alphabroder, your user login for their website determines the version of the price list file that will be downloaded to your website and there could be "many reasons" why an item is not included in the list. Fast Accurate Bids is only able to find the items that are actually in your version of the price list. You can still create bids for these items, however, by adding them to the Custom Items Page and using them from that source.

Adjusting the pricing

The pricing area is at the right side of the Design and Pricing Page. The top of this area shows the item costs. Select the cost category that is appropriate for the line item. For example, if you get case pricing from your supplier, make sure that **Case Cost** is selected.

When an item is added to the Design and Pricing page, the field **Set Shipping Charge** is set to $0.00. If you know that you will have to pay for shipping the items to your shop and you know the amount, then change the amount in **Set Shipping Charge** to that amount. If you are uncertain of the amount you'll have to pay for shipping, then select the radio button **Calculated Shipping** to add the estimated amount Fast Accurate Bids calculates to cover your shipping cost.

Check **Choose Tax Rate**, and if it needs to be changed, enter the correct rate for the order. For your convenience, Fast Accurate Bids provides a drop-down list of the last eight tax rates that have been entered.

The **Item Calculated Price** and **Total Calculated Price** fields show the pricing the Fast Accurate Bids software proposes. These prices are based on the choices you have made and the associated values on the Profile Settings Page. They are display fields and cannot be changed.

Fast Accurate Bids has been designed so that if your company takes the time to create a set of pricing profiles for your particular pricing policy, then almost all the line item entry will be done at this point and there will be no need to adjust the pricing.

1. Check the item cost fields and select the one to use for the bid.
2. Note the shipping fields, but leave shipping set to $0.00.
3. Check the tax rate field and select a rate to use for the bid.
4. Enter a discount, (e.g., enter **-10 %**.)
5. Click **Add to Line Items List**.

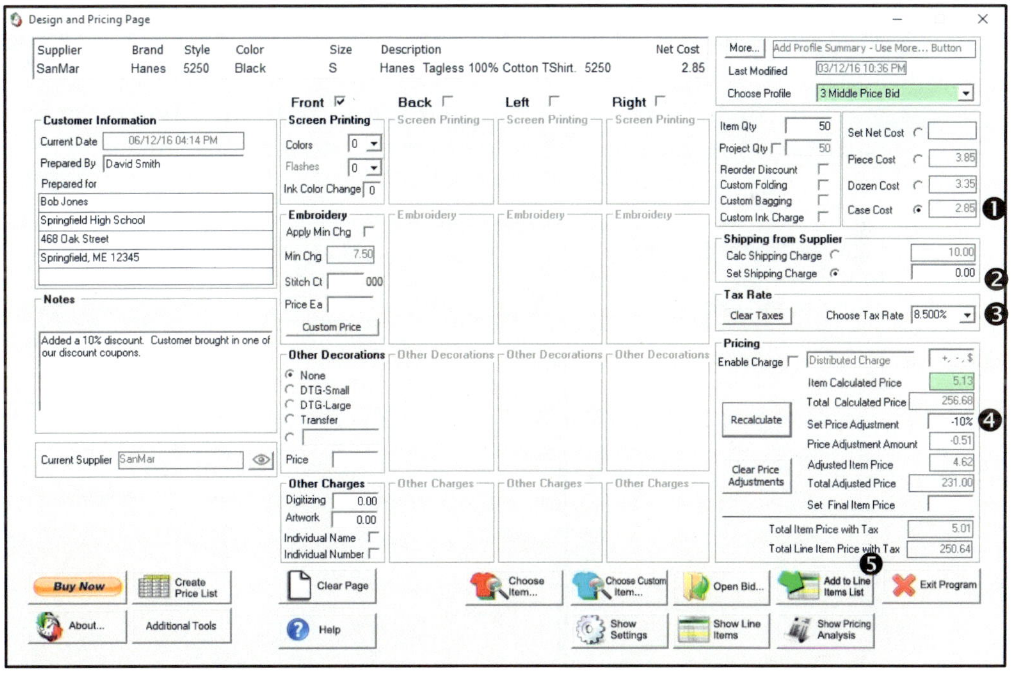

Things to note

- The **Set Net Cost** field lets you override the item cost. For example, if you get a good buy on a closeout from the supplier and you are willing to pass along this savings to your customer, this field can be used for entering the price at which you got the closeout items.

- The **Set Shipping Charge** is provided to recoup any charges you incur for having items shipped to you from your supplier. If you know what this charge is, you can enter the exact amount in this field. If you are uncertain about what shipping will cost you, you can use a calculated shipping amount by selecting **Calculated Shipping**.
- Fast Accurate Bids automatically updates the pricing fields whenever you make a change and then tab out of the field.
- The Fast Accurate Bids Pricing Analysis Page provides detailed information on the contribution of each charge and discount to the calculated price for the current line item. It provides a useful tool if you have questions regarding the calculated prices.
- Clicking the **Recalculate** button manually forces Fast Accurate Bids to calculate the prices based on the currently selected choices on this screen. This feature is convenient if you change the value in a field and would like to update the price information without actually tabbing out of the field.
- You can turn off and back on again the display of the item cost information by clicking the button with the eye icon ( ). This button is provided on the Design and Pricing Page, the Choose Item Page, and the Custom Item Page. Clicking it on any of these pages hides or shows the information for the other two pages as well. Consider hiding your item costs when you have a customer present while doing their bid.

Adding the item to the Line Items Page

When you clicked **Add to Line Items List** on the Design and Pricing Page, you completed the first line item for the bid.

1. Click the **Show Design and Pricing** button to return to the Design and Pricing Page.

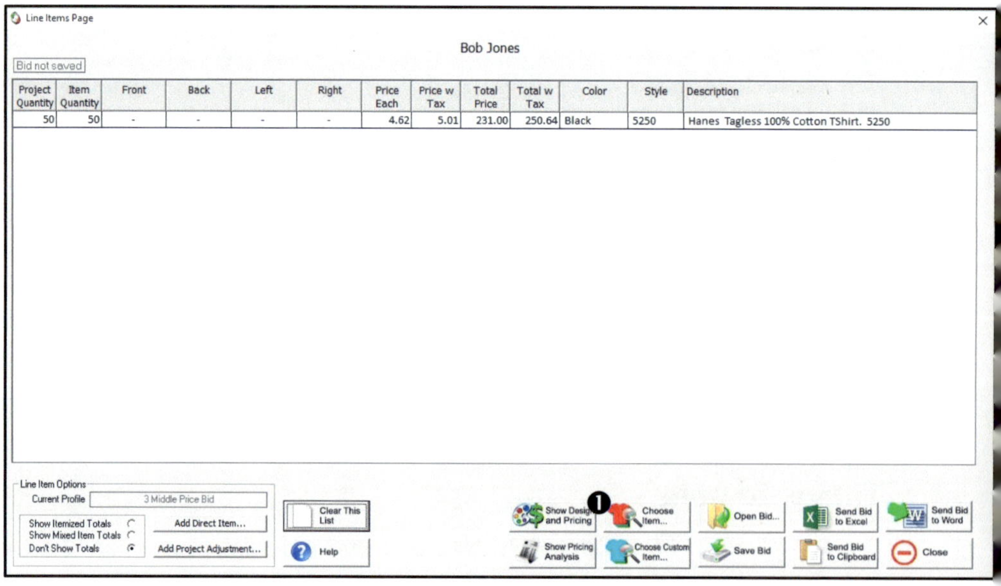

Things to note

- After you've entered a line item, if the next line item is for the same item ID, but with a different quantity or configuration, click the Show Design and Pricing Page button. If it's for a different item, which you can get via the Choose Item Page, click the Choose Item button. Otherwise, click the Add Custom Item button to access the Custom Item Page.
- Note that at the top of the Line Items Page, Fast Accurate Bids displays the customer name that you entered in the Prepared For field of the Design and Pricing Page. It also shows the file name for the bid whenever you are working with a bid that you have previously saved.
- You can sort the line items by clicking in the header field for the column you want to sort by. Currency and numeric files sort numerically. Text fields sort alphabetically.
- You can change the column widths on the Line Items Page by hovering the mouse over the column divider in the header row and dragging the divider to change the width.
- You can return the column widths to their default settings by right-clicking in any of the rows and selecting **Set Column Widths to Defaults** from the menu that appears.
- You can move individual line items up or down the Line Items List as described in the section in this manual called Moving Line Items.
- Each item on the Line Items List has stored within it a record of the settings used to create it. This means that if you decide to change a profile setting while making a bid, the change you make will be used for the subsequent line items, but not for the line items you added to the Line Items Page prior to the change. For additional information on working with saved bids see Pricing Profiles and Saved Bids.
- The columns **Front**, **Back**, **Left**, and **Right** provide information on the decorations for each of these areas. When you select more than one decoration choice on the Design and Pricing page (for example, if you select screen printing together with individual names and numbers), the term **Mixed** is shown to indicate a mix of decoration techniques.

Adding the next line items

To add another line item for the same item ID, e.g., where the only difference is the quantity, return to the Design and Pricing Page, change the item quantity, and then click **Add to Line Items List**.

1. Change the quantity for the item (e.g., **100**) and click **Add to Line Items List**.
2. The new line item is added to the list.
3. Repeat steps 1 through 3 above to add the third line item for 150 shirts.

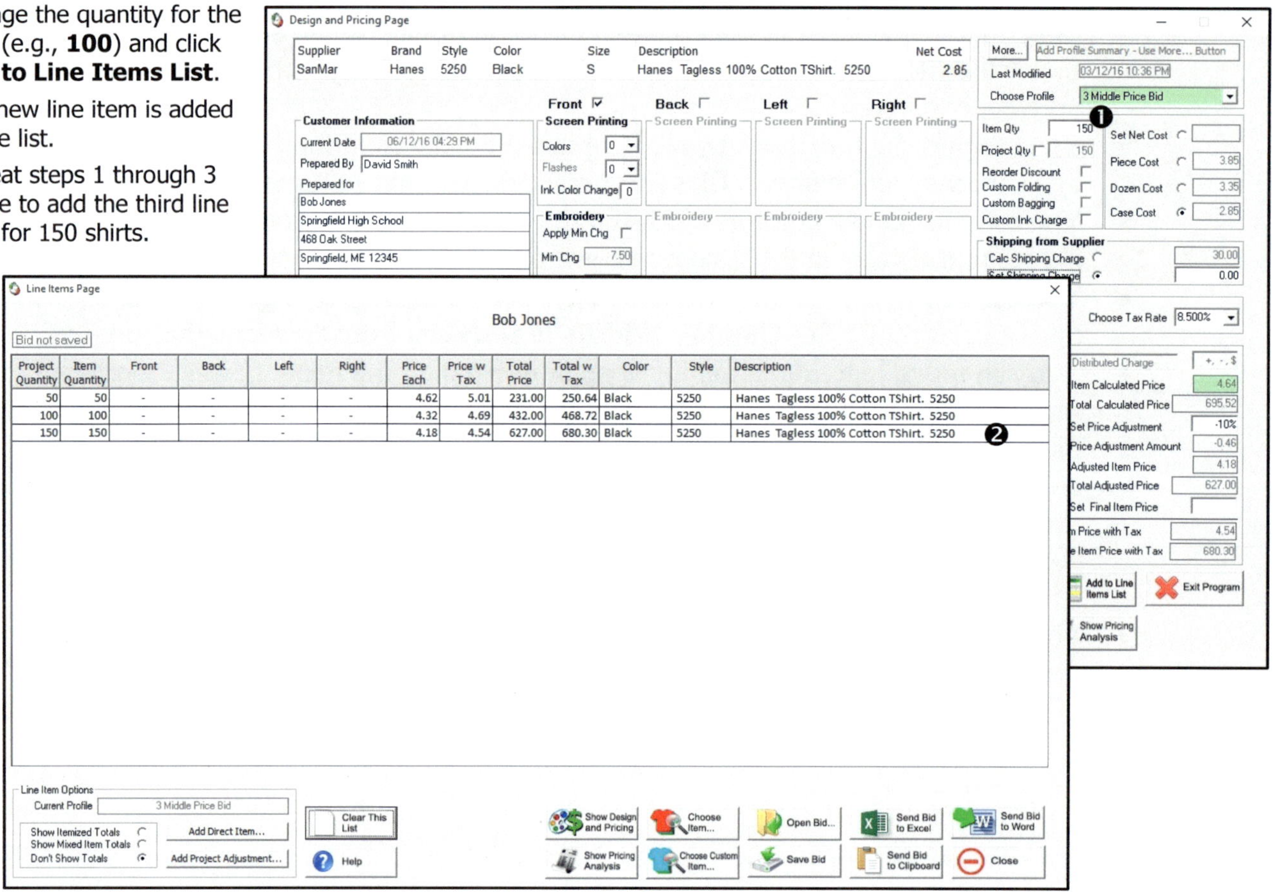

Things to note

- Because the Design and Pricing Page retains all its settings, it is very easy and efficient to respond to bid requests for a single item in an assortment of quantities.

Sending the line items table to Microsoft Word

Once the Line Items Page looks the way you want it to appear for the customer, finish the bid by sending the line items table for inclusion in the finished bid for the customer.

1. Click **Send Bid to Word**.

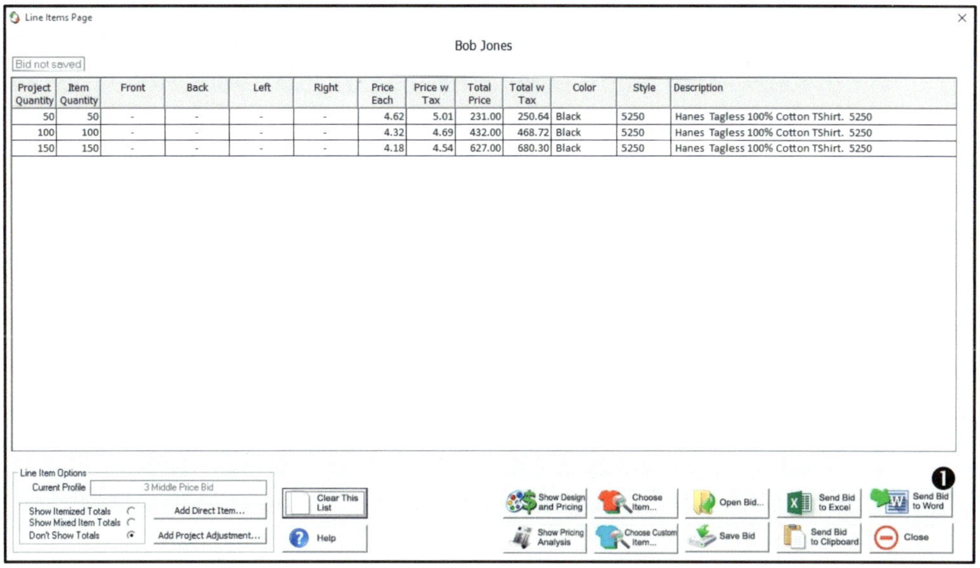

Things to note

- There are radio buttons at the lower left of the Line Items Page for adding a row to the line items list to show totals for the columns.
- When creating bids that itemize the charges, for example separate line items for screens, printing, shirts, etc., choose **Show Itemized Totals** to give your customer a total price each for items.
- When creating bids that are for an assortment of items printed with the same image, choose **Show Mixed Item Totals** since showing a total price each for items for these types of bids does not make sense.
- Clicking the **Add Project Adjustment** button opens a dialog box for adding an additional line item on the line items table. A project adjustment can be a specific amount or a percentage. This feature is intended to provide a means to add an adjustment to the entire bid as opposed to a single line item on the bid. For example, this field could be used to add a line for charging for a rush job. For information on using this feature, see the section in this manual called Adding a project adjustment.
- Clicking the **Add Direct Item** button opens a dialog box for adding an additional line item directly to the line items table. This feature is intended to provide a means to add separately itemized charges to the bid such as charges for screens, setup charges, and the like. For more information about direct line item charges, see Adding Direct Line Items.

- When you add an item using the **Add Direct Item** feature, the amount is exactly what you enter in the dialog box. Alternately, for line items that you add using the Design and Pricing Page, the amount of the item will be increased by the item overhead, checkin/layout, item markup, administrative overhead, and commission as specified on the associated pricing profile.
- If you want to remove a line item, right-click in the line, select **Delete Row** from the menu that appears, and click **Yes**, to the prompt to delete the row.
- If you want to hide a column on the line item table, right-click in the header for the column and select **Hide This Column**. This feature can be useful for making the line item list on the finished bid larger and easier to understand.
- To redisplay hidden columns, right-click in the header, and select **Show All Columns**.
- The right-click menu also provides choices for setting the column widths to fit the data and setting the column widths back to the default. Making the column widths smaller on the line items page will reduce the overall width of the line items table on the finished bid so that you can resize it to make it larger on the finished bid.
- One of the best ways to minimize the width of the line items list is to right-click and remove the columns that are not used for bid information. For example, if the job does not call for collecting sales tax on the job, the columns for **Price w Tax** and **Total w Tax** can be removed.
- To change a line item, click on it to bring it into the Design and Pricing Page, make the changes you want, send the changed version of line item to the Line Items Page, and delete the original version.
- If the **Send bid to Word** button is dimmed out, it means Fast Accurate Bids could not find a copy of Microsoft Word 2007 or later on your computer. If this is the case, you can use the **Send Bid to Clipboard** button on the Line Items Page to copy the line items table into any document that you can use the Windows Paste function.
- When you want to start another bid, click the Clear List button on the Line Items Page.
- If you use Microsoft Office 365, Word must be open on your computer for Fast Accurate Bids to successfully create the finished bid.

Finishing the bid in Microsoft Word

When you click **Send Bid to Word**, the finished bid, which opens automatically, includes the date, customer name and address, and the line items table.

You can edit the text to add or change anything that you want. The file for the finished bid behaves just as any other file created in Word. There are no Fast Accurate Bids controls manipulating it. You can edit the text and save the file to any location on your system that you choose. Depending on the capabilities of your Word software, you can save the file as a Word file or PDF to send to the customer, print it, or copy the text and paste it into an email.

To finish the bid,

1. Enter information in the **Re:** line.
2. Replace any placeholder text with the information you want.
3. Save the finished bid.

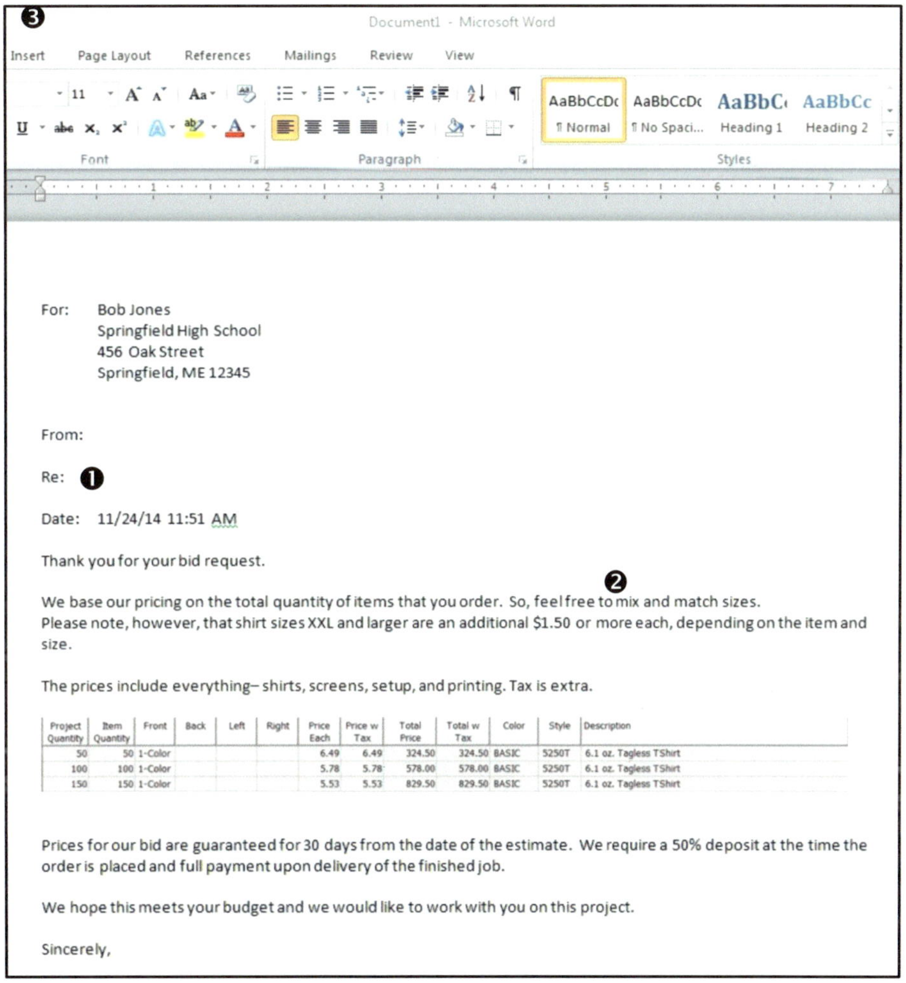

For: Bob Jones
Springfield High School
456 Oak Street
Springfield, ME 12345

From:

Re:

Date: 11/24/14 11:51 AM

Thank you for your bid request.

We base our pricing on the total quantity of items that you order. So, feel free to mix and match sizes.
Please note, however, that shirt sizes XXL and larger are an additional $1.50 or more each, depending on the item and size.

The prices include everything– shirts, screens, setup, and printing. Tax is extra.

Project Quantity	Item Quantity	Front	Back	Left	Right	Price Each	Price w Tax	Total Price	Total w Tax	Color	Style	Description
50	50	1-Color				6.49	6.49	324.50	324.50	BASIC	5250T	6.1 oz. Tagless TShirt
100	100	1-Color				5.78	5.78	578.00	578.00	BASIC	5250T	6.1 oz. Tagless TShirt
150	150	1-Color				5.53	5.53	829.50	829.50	BASIC	5250T	6.1 oz. Tagless TShirt

Prices for our bid are guaranteed for 30 days from the date of the estimate. We require a 50% deposit at the time the order is placed and full payment upon delivery of the finished job.

We hope this meets your budget and we would like to work with you on this project.

Sincerely,

Things to note

- The line items table is a non-editable image. This protects you from the possibility of any changes being made to this information.
- The Fast Accurate Bids bid template is a standard Word template. The *Fast Accurate Bids Shop Owner's Manual* describes how to open the template file and customize it for your business.
- If you'd prefer to work with an editable version of the Line Items List, click the button on the Line Items Page to send the bid to Microsoft Excel.

Saving the bid file

In addition to saving the finished bid as a Microsoft Word file, the Line Items Page lets you save the bid itself and also open previously saved bids for editing. You can save bid information any time that you want, but it's especially important to save this information just after you finish a bid so that you have an accurate record of the data for the bid you sent to your customer.

To save a bid file,

1. Click **Save Bid**.
2. Create a file name for the bid.
3. Click **Save**.
4. Click **Save** to the confirmation message.

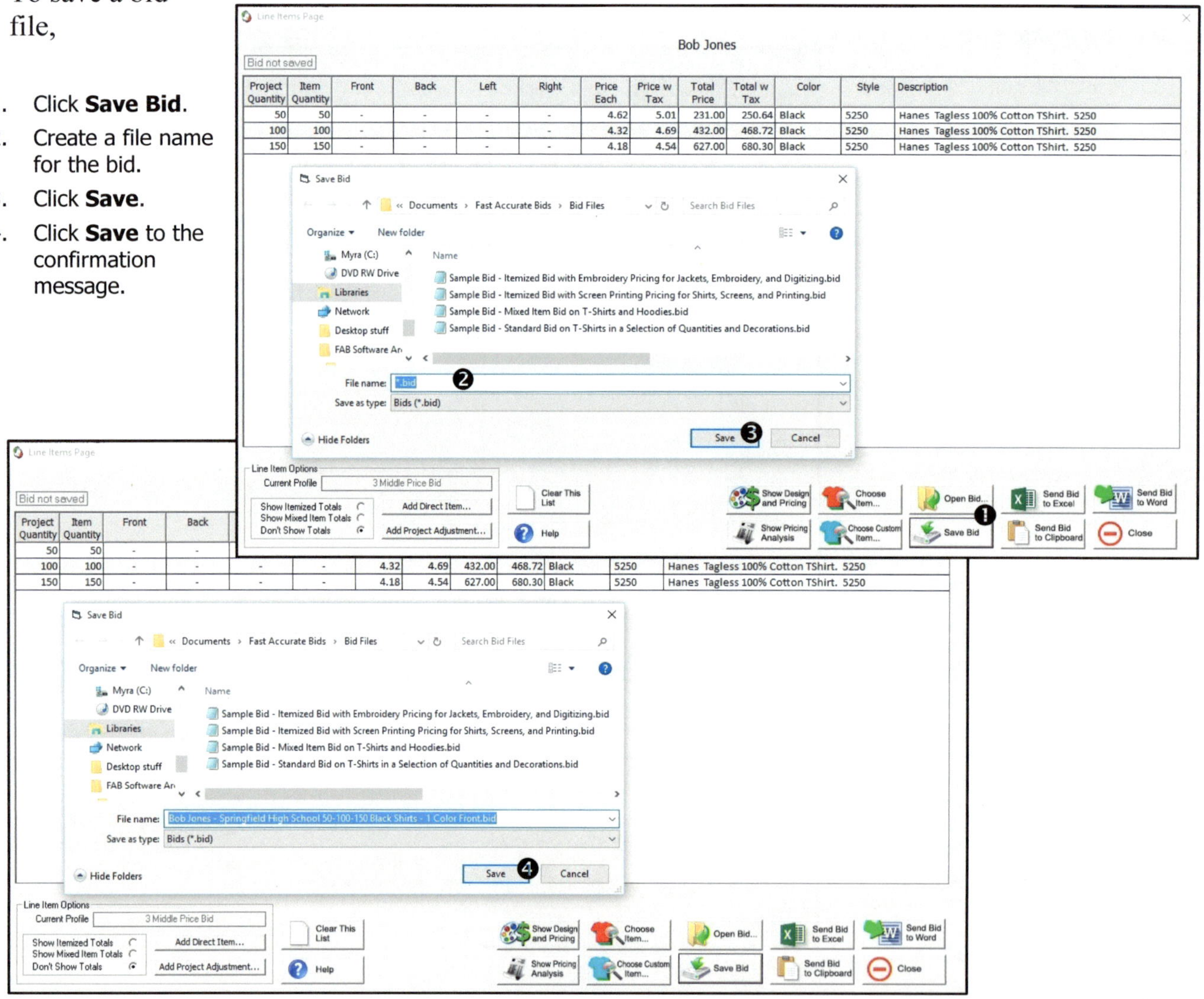

Note: Fast Accurate Bids automatically adds the file extension **.bid** to bid files. You do not need to add this information; in fact, adding it would result in a file name that ends in **.bid.bid**.

For more information about saving and restoring bids, see the section in this manual called Saving and restoring bids.

Adding Custom Items to a Bid

The Custom Items Page lets you add an item to a bid that you cannot get by selecting it from the Choose Item Page. To see the Custom Items Page, click the **Show Custom Item** button on the Design and Pricing Page.

You can add an item on-the-fly to the Custom Item page by clicking the Add Row button and entering the item information in the blank row that appears at the top of the main table on the page. The only required field is **Style**, but if you do not add information in the other fields, the corresponding fields will be blank when you send the information to the Line Items Page.

You can send an item to the Design and Pricing Page by either clicking the **Send to Design and Pricing** button or right-clicking and choosing **Send to Design and Pricing** from the menu that appears.

When you send a custom item to the Design and Pricing, Fast Accurate Bids automatically saves list and closes the Custom Items Page for you.

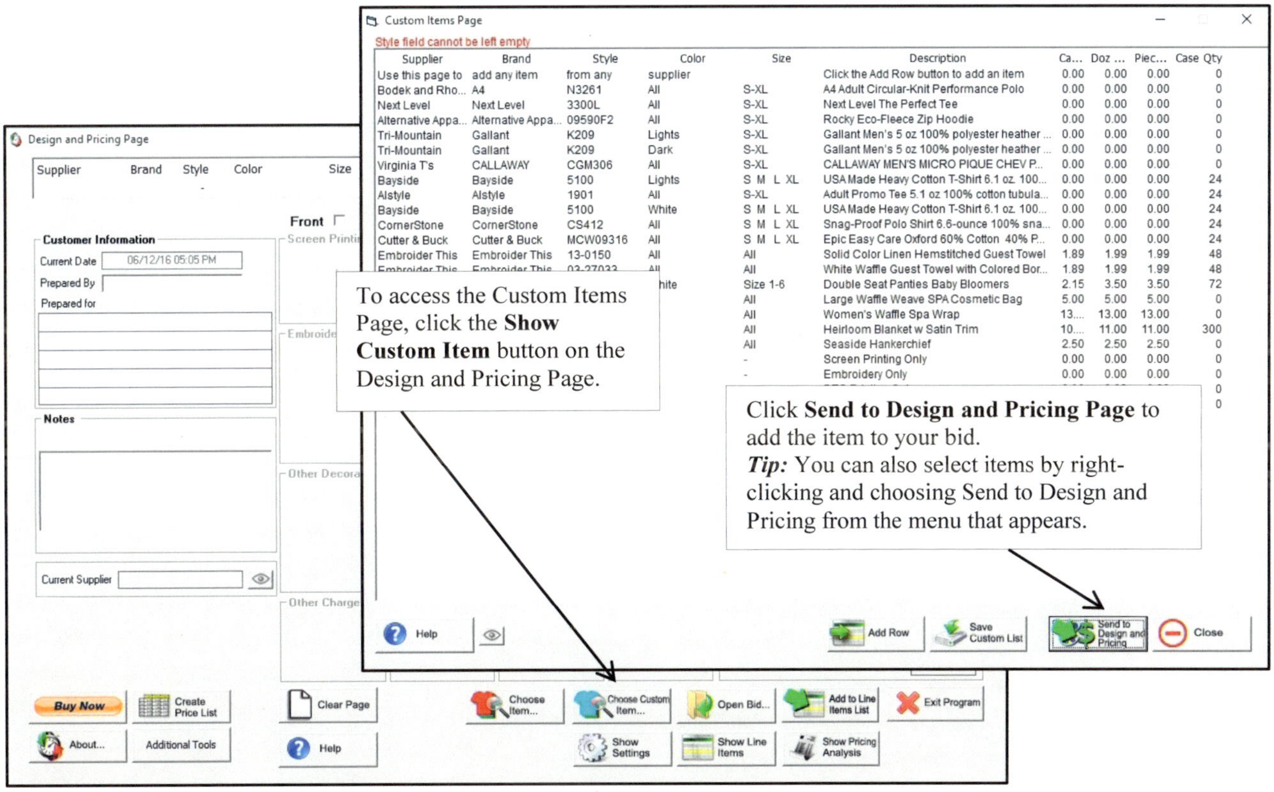

Things to note

- You can sort the information on the Custom Item Page, by clicking in the column heading of the column to sort by.

- Once you add the item to the Design and Pricing Page, the program treats the custom item in the same manner as an item selected from the Choose Item Page.
- To delete a row, right-click in the row you want to delete and select **Delete row** from the menu that appears.
- Consider creating a custom item for use when printing items supplied by your customer. Enter **Customer** as the style, leave **Item Cost** set to $0.00 and enter **Items supplied by customer** as the description.
- When entering a custom item and then using it immediately, keep in mind that the software automatically advances you to the next line of the table when you tab out of the **Case Qty** field. Make sure that your cursor is in the line that you want added to your bid so that you don't inadvertently send the wrong custom item to the Design and Pricing Page.

Editing the Description, Color and other current item fields

To edit the current items fields on the Design and Pricing Page click in the field and make the change you want. The changes you make to the description are carried forward to the Line Items Page but they do not change the information on the Choose Item Page.

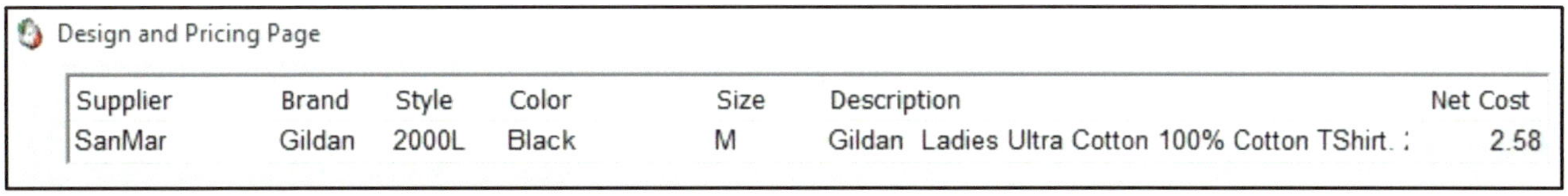

For items that you choose from the Custom Item Page, you can also edit the information for any of the fields from within the Custom Item Page.

The only field that cannot be directly edited in this manner is **Net Cost**. To change the net cost for an item, selecting the pricing choice **Set Item Cost** and enter the net cost you want used.

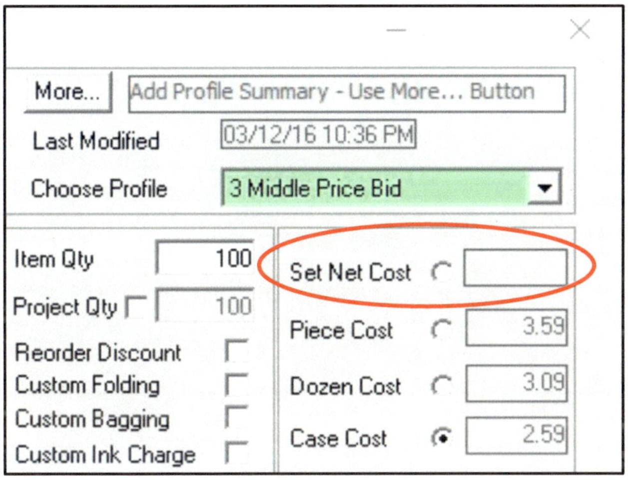

Screen Printing Charges

To select decoration tasks for screen printing, begin by selecting the check boxes for the areas to decorate, (i.e., **Front**, **Back**, **Left**, or **Right**). The choices for screen printing decoration are just below the decoration area choices.

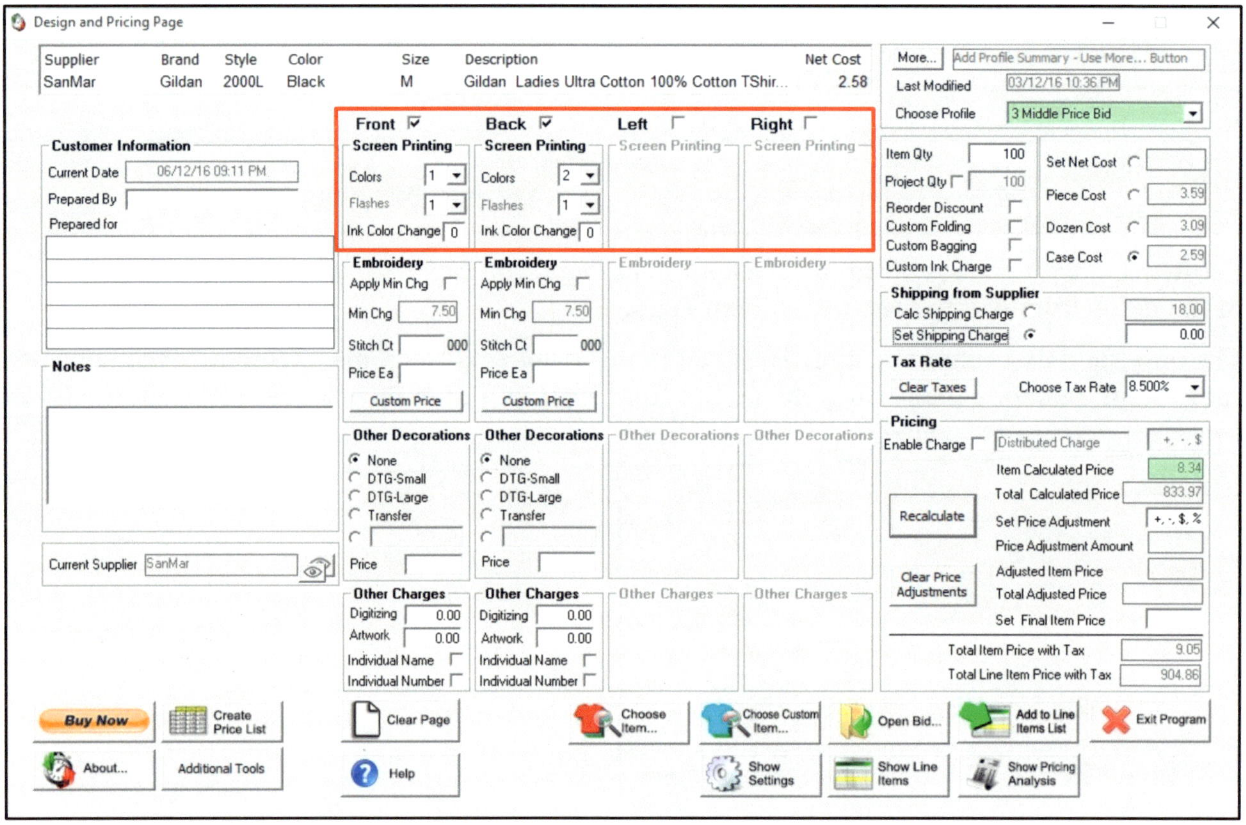

Enter the number of colors for the design by clicking the down-arrow and selecting it from the list that appears. You can select the number of flashes in the same way.

If the customer requests changing one or more of the ink colors for some of the items, enter the number of color changes requested in the field **Ink Color Change**. This charge is intended to cover the time it takes to clean the screen and reset it on the press.

Embroidery Charges

To select decoration tasks for embroidery, begin by selecting the checkbox for the area to decorate, (i.e., **Front**, **Back**, **Left**, or **Right)**. The choices for embroidery decoration are just below the screen printing choices.

The field **Min Chg** displays your minimum charge amount for embroidery. The amount in this field is always shown. The field **Price Ea** displays the price that will be charged for the embroidery.

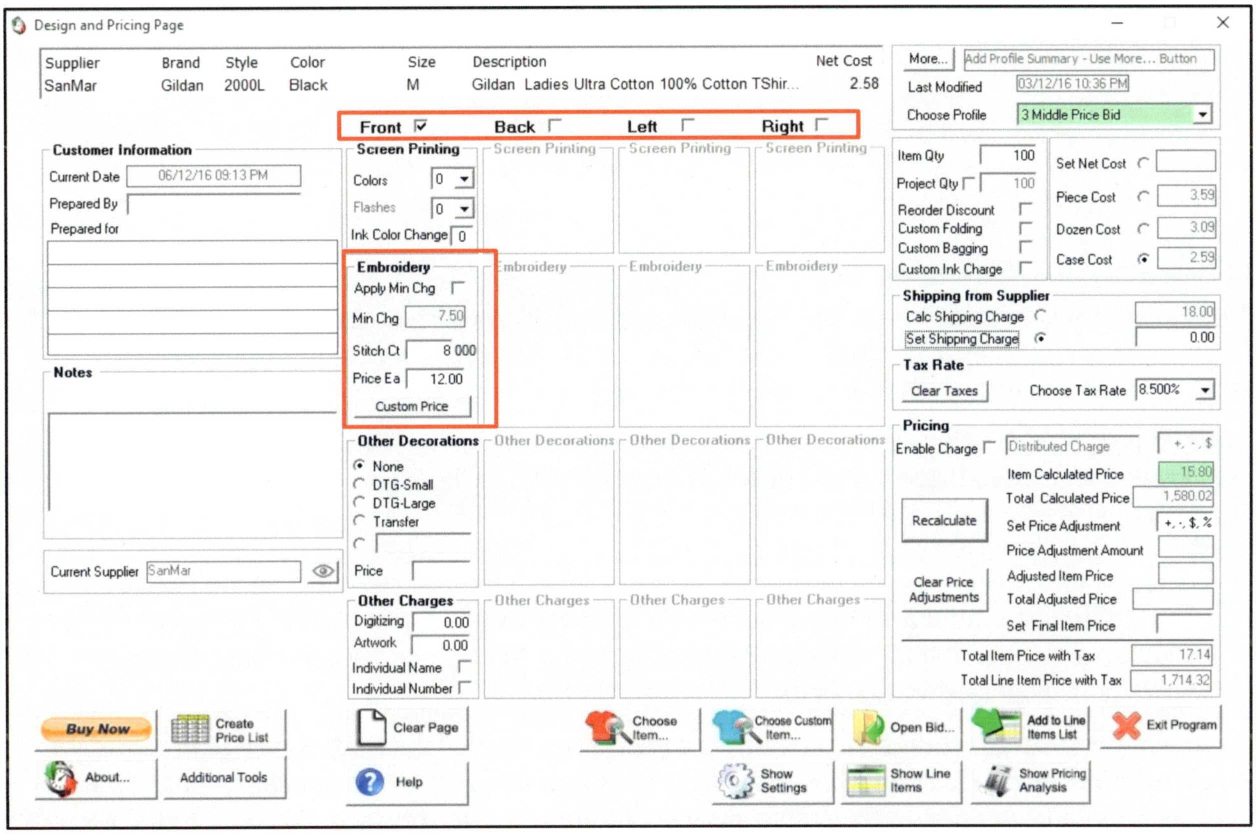

There are several ways you can specify the charge for embroidery. Each of these methods is described below.

Embroidery Minimum Charge

The Apply Min Chg check box lets you quickly set the price for small embroidery tasks to the minimum that you charge.

When the Embroidery Minimum Charge check box is selected, the amount for the minimum charge is displayed in the field **Price Ea** and the pricing choices for **Stitch Ct** and **Custom Price** are deactivated. To reactivate the other pricing choices, unselect the **Apply Min Chg** check box.

Embroidery Stitch Ct

The field **Stitch Ct** allows you to enter the number of stitches in the embroidery design to get a calculated charge amount. The number you enter in this field is multiplied by 1,000 and by the amount in the field **Price/1000 Stitches** on the Profile Settings Page.

When the Apply Min Chg check box is selected, the field **Stitch Ct** is deactivated. To reactivate **Stitch Ct**, unselect the Apply Min Chg check box.

Embroidery Custom Price

When you select **Custom Price,** the Add Embroidery Custom Price dialog box appears to let you to enter the cost and a markup you want for the embroidery.

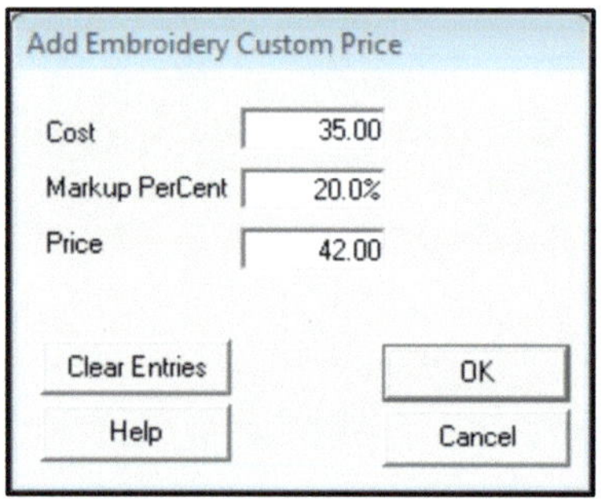

You do not need to enter the price. The price is calculated based on the amounts you enter in the fields **Cost** and **Markup Percent**. This feature can be particularly useful if you use a subcontractor for your embroidery orders.

When the Apply Min Chg check box is selected, Custom Price button is deactivated. To reactivate the Custom Price button, unselect the Apply Min Chg check box.

Price Ea

If you know the price you want to charge for the embroidery, you can click in the field **Price Ea** and enter it directly. When using one of the other methods to enter the price for an embroidery, the calculated price is displayed in this field. The price that will be used for the embroidery will be whatever is displayed in this field.

Note: On the Profile Settings Page, there is a check box labeled **Exclude Overhead Charges** that lets you control whether check in and layout, administrative overhead and commission charges should be applied to the embroidery decoration charge shown in the field **Price Ea**. For more information, see the *Fast Accurate Bids Shop Owner's Manual.*

Other Decorations

To select other decoration tasks, begin by selecting the check box for the area to decorate, (i.e., **Front**, **Back**, **Left**, or **Right**). The choices for Other Decorations are just below the embroidery choices.

The choices for the Other Decorations come from the pricing profile currently used. The Other Decorations choices for the built-in pricing profiles are DTG – Small, DTG – Large, and Transfer. On the Design and Pricing Page, there is an additional choice that provides a blank field next to it so that you can enter a decoration task on-the-fly as you're doing a bid.

The field **Price** is initially blank. When you choose one of the decoration techniques, it displays the price that will be charged for the decoration you choose.

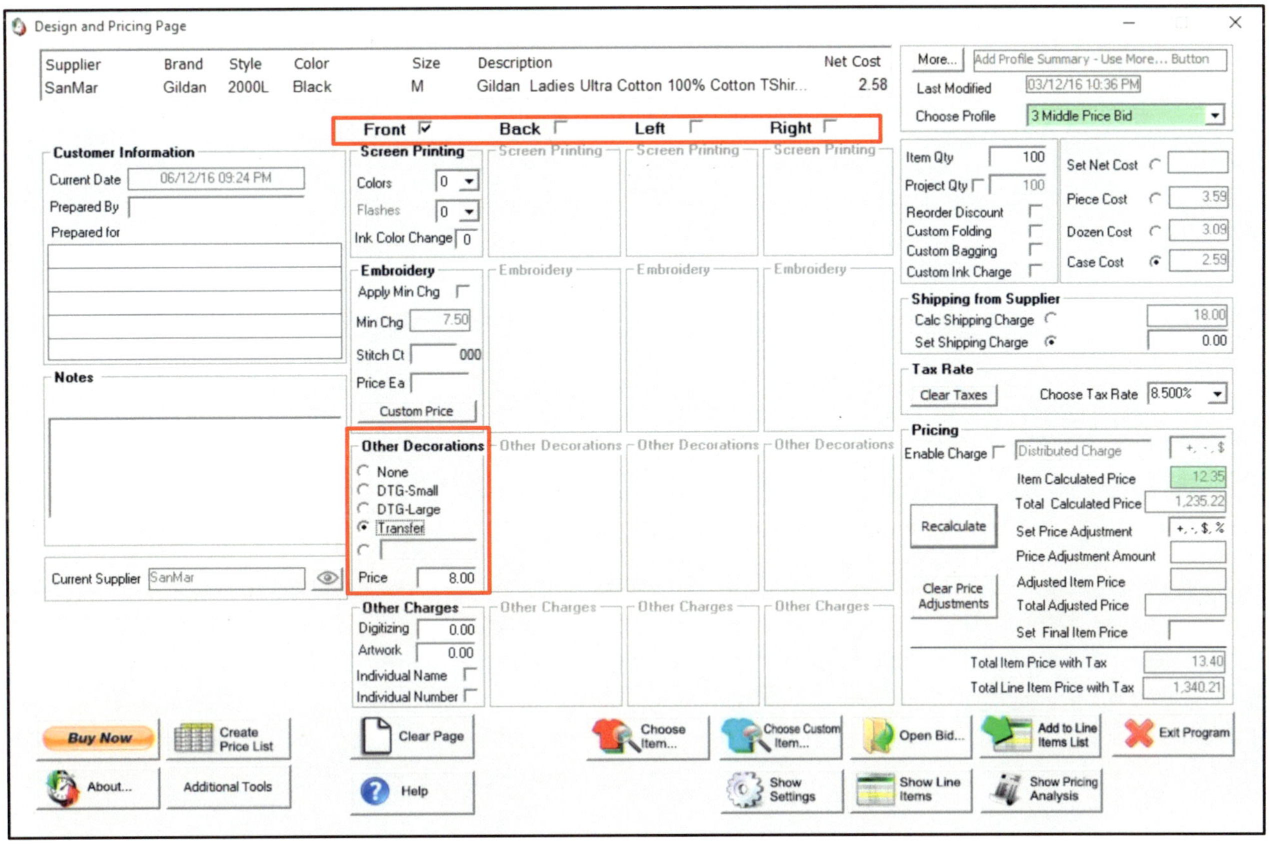

Other Decoration pre-set choices

The labels that appear for the Other Decoration choices are taken from the current pricing profile. For this reason you may see different choices depending on the pricing profile you're using.

The choice for **None** allows you to clear the Other Decoration area, if you select one of the pre-set choices and then decide that you do not want to use any of the Other Decoration choices.

Note: On the Profile Settings Page, there is a check box labeled **Exclude Overhead Charges** that lets you control whether check in and layout, administrative overhead and commission charges should be applied to the other decoration charge shown in the field **Price Ea**. For more information, see the *Fast Accurate Bids Shop Owner's Manual*.

Other Decoration blank field

The blank field in the Other Decoration area allows you to enter whatever label that you want for a decoration technique and the amount that you want to charge for it in the **Price** field below it.

This choice can be useful for entering a decoration technique on-the-fly. It can also be useful as a simple means of overriding the amount that you want to charge for a decoration. For example, suppose the pricing profile you want to use for the line item sets the price for Vinyl at $5, but you want to charge $8.50. To do so, select the last choice for Other Decoration, enter **Vinyl** in the blank field associated with this choice, and enter $8.50 in the field **Price**.

Other charges on bids

There are four areas where you can enter other charges on bids. These are:

- The Other Charges area
- The check boxes just below the quantity fields
- The Shipping from Supplier area
- The **Distributed Charge** field

This section describes the Other Charges section and the check boxes just below the quantity fields. For information on charges for shipping from your supplier, see Changing the Shipping Charge. For information on the field **Distributed Charge**, see Distributed Charge.

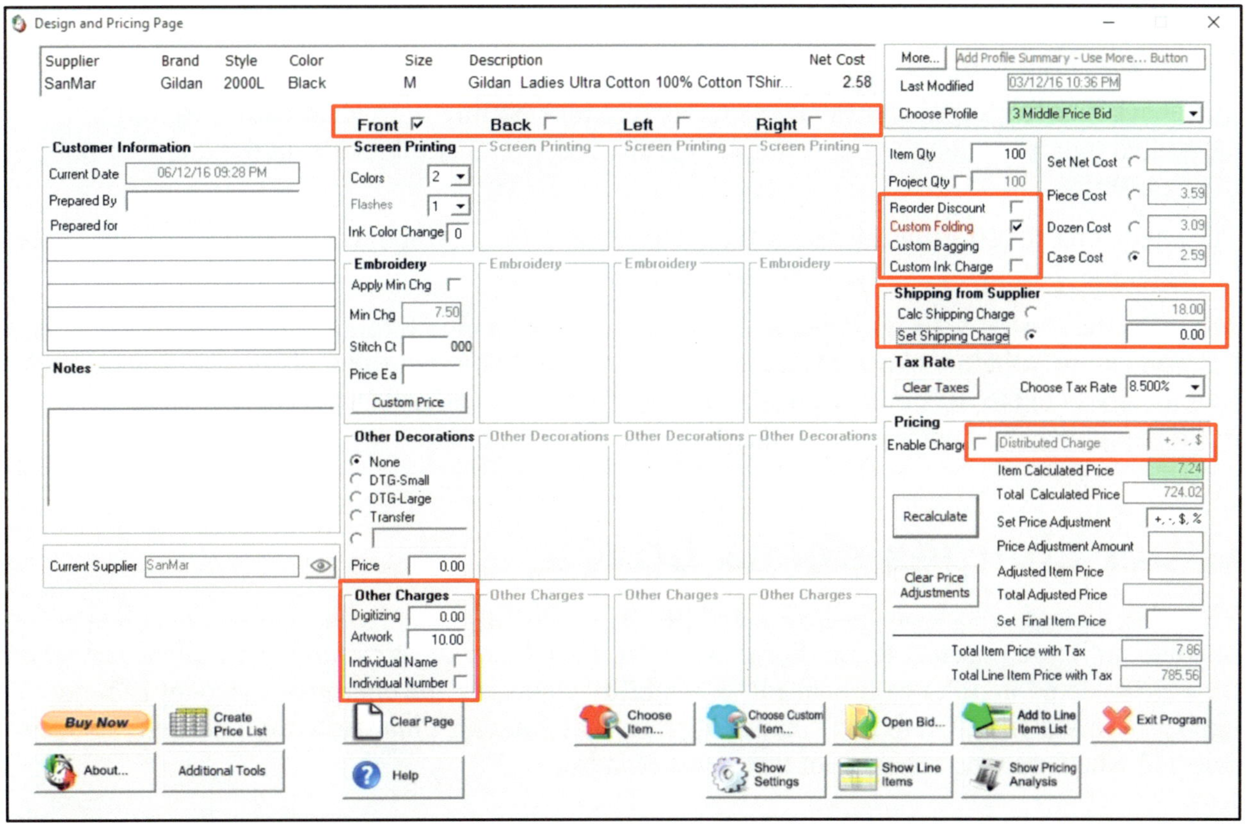

Other Charges area

The Other Charges area appears at the bottom of the list of decoration choices. If you don't see these choices, click the check box for the associated decoration area near the top of the Design and Pricing Page (i.e., **Front**, **Back**, **Left**, **and Right**).

The Other Charges area provides the field **Digitizing** for charges for digitizing embroidery designs and the field **Artwork** for charges for artwork for any type of decoration.

Digitizing

The field **Digitizing** is intended for covering the cost of digitizing artwork for embroidery.

Note: Fast Accurate Bids does not apply checkin/layout, administrative overhead or commission to the field **Digitizing**. The amount you enter in this field will be the amount charged the customer.

Artwork

The field **Artwork** is intended for covering the cost of helping the customer with artwork for any type of job whether it's screen printing, embroidery, DTG, etc.

Many apparel decorators do not charge extra for simple assistance on artwork. It's a good idea to have a guideline in mind for your business regarding the amount of artwork assistance you are willing to provide at no cost to your customers.

Note: Fast Accurate Bids does not apply checkin/layout, administrative overhead or commission to the field **Artwork**. The amount you enter in this field will be the amount charged the customer.

Name and Number

The check box for **Name** allows you a charge extra for putting individual names (or any individual words) on items. For example, putting individual employee's names and their job titles on shirts.

The check box for **Number** allows you to charge extra for putting individual numbers on items. For example, putting individual numbers on athletic shirts.

Note: On the Profile Settings Page, there is a check box labeled Exclude Overhead Charges that lets you control whether check in and layout, administrative overhead and commission charges should be applied to the other decoration charge shown in the field **Price Ea**. For more information, see the *Fast Accurate Bids Shop Owner's Manual*.

Other charges check boxes

The other charges check boxes are located just below the quantity fields. These check boxes stay selected until you unselect them. For this reason, Fast Accurate Bids turns their labels red when they are selected in order to enhance their visibility whenever the charge or discount is being applied. This is intended to call you attention so that you don't inadvertently leave any of them selected when creating subsequent line items on a bid.

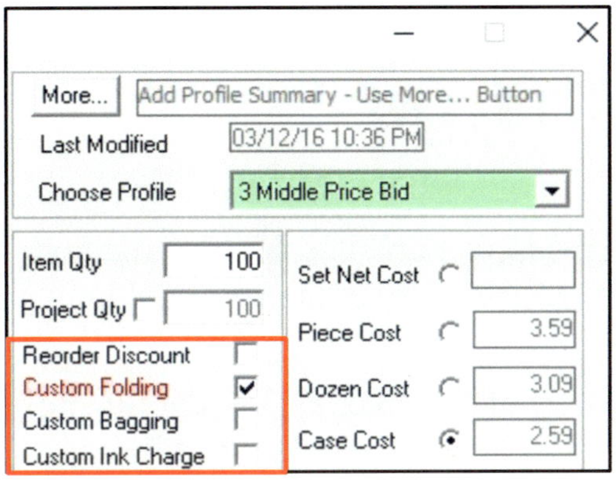

Reorder Discount

The **Reorder Discount** is provided to pass along to the customer the saving from not having to prepare new screens for a repeat job.

Custom Folding

The **Custom Folding** check box allows you to record a charge in cases where the customer asks to have the finished items individually folded or otherwise given special handling.

Custom Bagging

The **Custom Bagging** check box allows you to add a charge for individually bagging finished items. This amount covers your cost of the bag and the time it takes to fold, insert, and seal the item in the bag.

Custom Ink Charge

The **Custom Ink Charge** check box is provided because an additive must be added to ink for jobs such as discharge printing and printing on nylon items and, after printing, the unused ink is no longer usable for other printing jobs and must be discarded.

Changing the Shipping Charge

Because shipping charges can vary greatly depending on the supplier and the shipping method, Fast Accurate Bids gives you control over how much to include on bids for the cost of shipping items from your supplier to your shop.

Unless you change it, the shipping charge is $0.00. However, you can enter an amount for shipping in the field **Set Shipping Charge**. You can also select the radio button **Calculated Shipping** to use the program's automatically calculated amount to cover the shipping. This amount is determined using the pricing profile fields **Supplier Min Shipping** and **Supplier Shipping**.

The calculation for this charge is the higher of either:

Supplier Shipping x Net Item Cost x Item Qty

Or, the amount specified in the field **Supplier Min Shipping.**

To enter a specific shipping charge, make sure the radio button next to the **Set Shipping Charge** field is selected, then enter the amount you want used for the shipping.

When you change the shipping charge to a different amount, the new amount persists in the **Set Shipping Charge** field until you either change it or close and reopen the program. When you close and reopen the program, the value for **Set Shipping Charge** resets to $0.00.

When you select **Calculated Shipping**, the program only applies the calculated shipping to the current line item and reverts back to **Set Shipping Charge** when the line item is added to the Line Items Page or a new item ID is sent to the Design and Pricing Page.

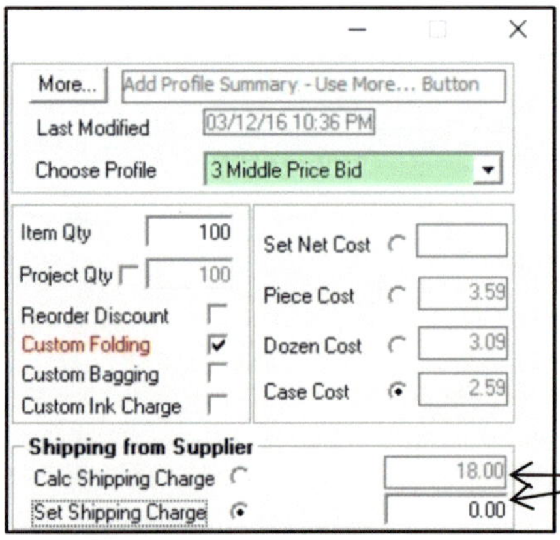

The calculated shipping amount is not used unless its radio button is selected.

When the **Set Shipping Charge** radio button is selected, you can enter whatever shipping amount you want used for the line item.

Things to note

- If you need to add a shipping charge for shipping the finished job to the customer, you can do so on the Line Items Page by adding a direct item for shipping.
- When applying a shipping charge, the amount charged is based on the item quantity for the line item. This means that when you have a mixed item bid, the cost for shipping the items to your shop is distributed correctly to each of the different types of items for the bid.

Changing the Tax Rate

The **Choose Tax Rate** field displays the tax rate for calculating the sales tax. As you make sales in taxing jurisdictions that have different tax rates, you can enter the new rate by selecting the rate in the field and changing it.

If you choose a different tax rate for a bid, the new rate is used until you either change it, or click **Clear Rates**.

Note: The **Choose Tax Rate** field retains a list of the last seven tax rates used in the order they were entered. Clicking the **Clear Tax Rates** button will remove all the tax rates entered so that you can build the list again.

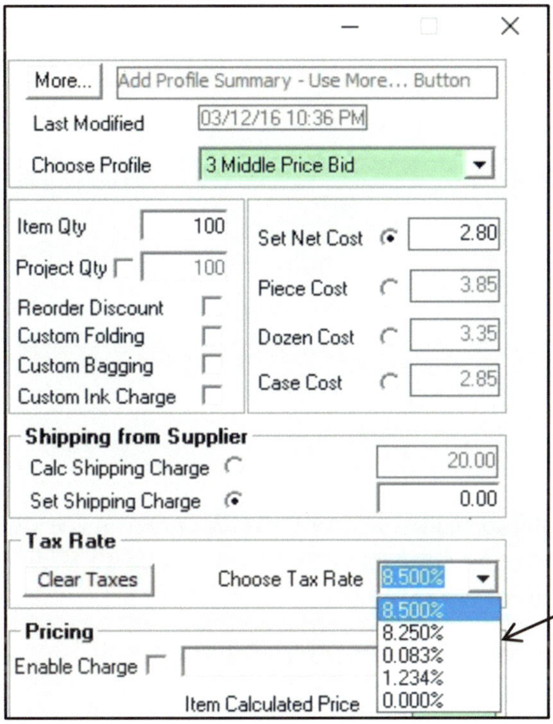

For your convenience, Fast Accurate Bids software retains the tax rate settings for the last seven tax rates entered.

Click the arrow to the right of the field to select a tax rate from the dropdown list that appears.

Adjusting Item Pricing

Taking the time to understand your pricing profiles and work with them until they accurately reflect your business will save significant time in creating bids. Moreover, it will allow you to trust the accuracy of the bids you create and ensure pricing consistency for your company.

Fast Accurate Bids is optimized for creating bids quickly and simply. The pricing display fields on the Design and Pricing Page show the individual item price and the total line item price. As you select decoration tasks, you can see the calculated prices increment. Both the **Item Calculated Price** field and the **Total Calculated Price** fields are updated whenever you make a change on this page that affects the calculated amounts.

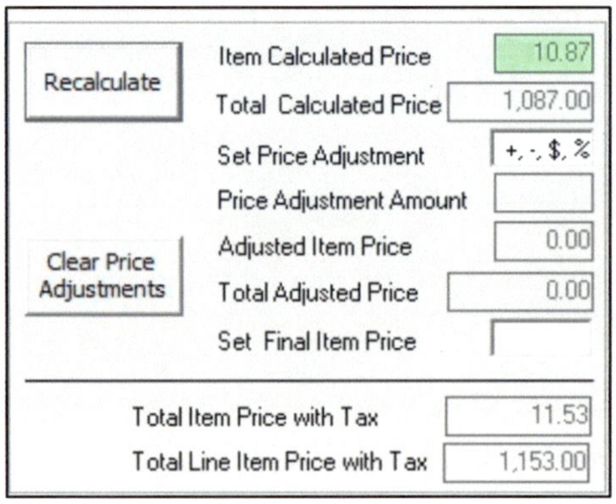

Note: At some point you may notice that the item calculated price, without any decorations or other charges selected, is still greater than the item cost. The reason for this is that Fast Accurate Bids has already applied charges such as the item markup to the item cost.

The sections that follow describe each of the price adjustment features provided in the software. You can adjust item pricing in the following ways:

- Change the item cost
- Add a distributed charge
- Adjust the calculated price by an amount or a percent
- Set a final item price

Changing the cost for an item

When you look up an item on the Choose Item Page and then send it to the Design and Pricing Page, the item cost information is taken from the supplier's pricing file.

The amount displayed for the item cost at the top of the page is determined by the pricing choice selected. The prices for **Piece Cost**, **Dozen Cost**, or **Case Cost** come from the data in the supplier's pricing file.

The choice **Set Net Cost** lets you override these prices and enter whatever price you want as the cost for the item. To do so, select the radio button next to the **Set Net Cost** field and enter the item cost that you want to use for the bid.

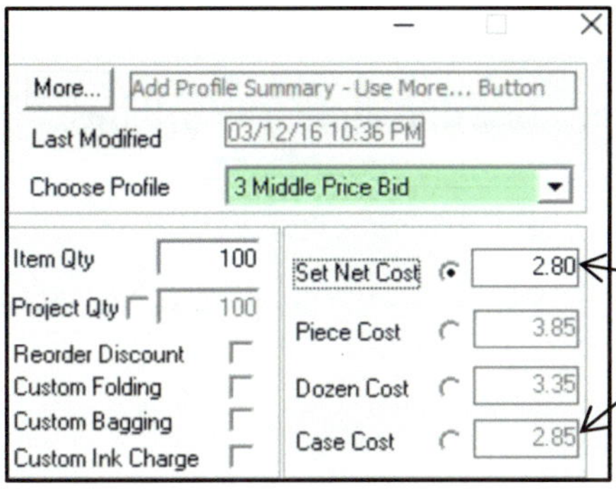

The item cost is based on the selected radio button.

The choice **Set Net Cost** allows you to override your supplier's pricing and set the item cost to what you want.

Note: The Show/Hide Item Costs button ( ), which is available on the Design and Pricing, Choose Item, and Custom Item Pages that lets you show or hide the item cost from those pages. This button is intended to provide you with a convenient way to hide your item costs when you have a customer looking over your shoulder as you do bids.

Adding a Distributed Charge

The field just below **Choose Tax Rate** is a user-definable field that has the temporary label **Distributed Charge**. This field is intended for the cost for items or services that you want to pass along to the customer.

For example, suppose you want to recoup your cost for a container of expensive specialty ink that costs $60 and the project quantity is 100. Then, the amount added to each item for the distributed charge will be $0.60.

Note: When you add a distributed charge the amounts in the fields **Item Calculated Price** and **Total Calculated Price** increase by more than just the distributed charge amount. The reason for this is that your administrative overhead and commission percentages are applied to the distributed charge amount.

To add a distributed charge,

1. Select the check box to activate the field.
2. Change the field label to whatever you want.
3. Enter the amount of the charge.

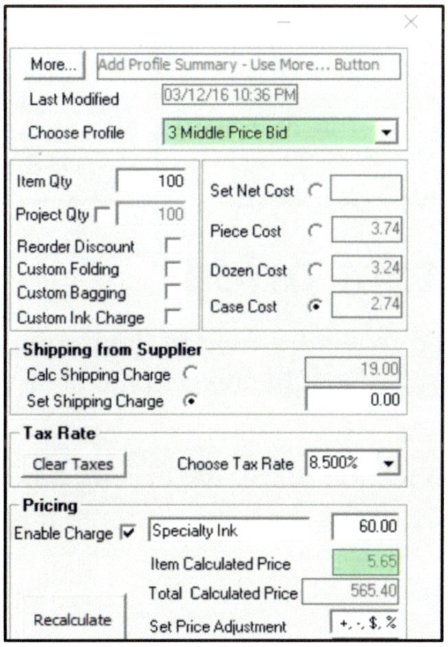

Things to note

- The user-defined **(Distributed Charge)** field is for adjustments to specific line items. To add an adjustment that pertains to all line items on the bid, use the Add Project Adjustment feature as described in Adding a Project Adjustment.
- If you use the **Distributed Charge** field to apply more than one adjustment to pricing, consider entering **See Notes** as the label for the field, and making a record of the adjustments it applies to in the **Notes** field at the left side of the Design and Pricing Page.
- You can enter a distributed charge as a specific amount or as a percent and as a positive or negative number. For example, to enter a percentage discount, enter a minus sign in front of the number and a percent sign after it.

Adjusting the calculated price

The calculated price is displayed with a light green background on the Design and Pricing Page. This is the suggested price for the line item based on the item's cost, the decoration tasks, the quantity, and the settings taken from the currently active pricing profile.

If the pricing profiles you use provide an accurate reflection of your pricing policies, then in most cases, you will not need to override the calculated price. Fast Accurate Bids does, however, provide the **Set Price Adjustment** field so that you can override the calculated price by an amount or percent that you specify.

You can enter an adjustment as a specific amount or as a percent and as a positive or negative number. For example, to enter a percentage discount, enter a minus sign in front of the number and a percent sign after it.

Fast Accurate Bids displays the new price in the **Adjusted Item Price** field.

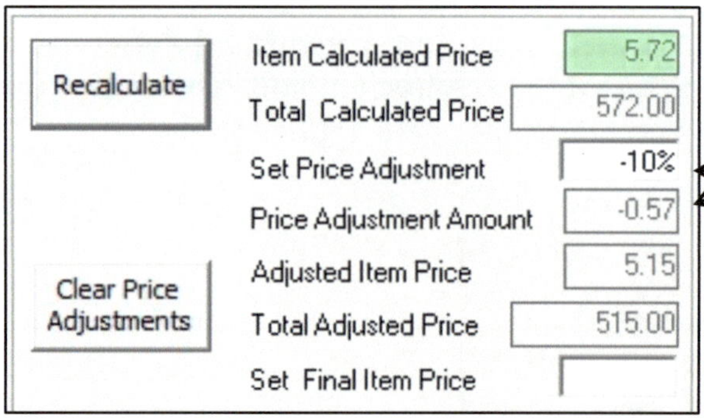

If you enter the adjustment as a percent, then the Price Adjustment Amount field displays the resulting amount of the adjustment. If you enter the adjustment as amount, then it displays the per cent that the amount comes to.

These are both display fields and can only be changed by changing the amount or percentage in the field **Set Price Adjustment.**

Setting a final item price

Set Final Item Price, the last direct entry field in the Pricing and Adjustments area, lets you override the calculations and specify right down to the penny what you want the bid amount per item to be.

The intention of this field is to let you tweak the pricing based on your business judgment about what's best for the sale. For example, for some customers you may choose to round a price such as $6.03 either up to $6.05 or possibly down to $6.00. For other customers, you may choose to change it to $5.97. It's entirely up to you.

Fast Accurate Bids provides you with an accurately calculated price but gives you complete control over the decision regarding the price you present to the customer.

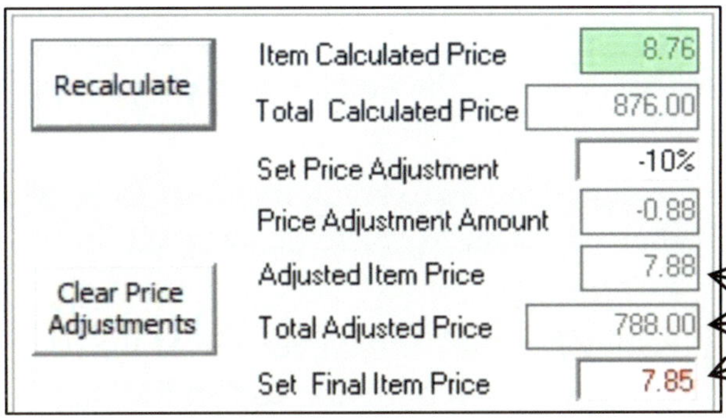

When you set a final price that is lower than the calculated price, the amount in the field **Set Final Item Price** turns red when you tab out of the field.

Note: When you use **Set Final Price** to override the calculated price, the Pricing Analysis Page still shows the complete calculated pricing and also lists the set customer price so that you have a record of how you arrived and the price for the line item.

Editing line items

The rows on the Line Items List are read-only. When you click in a row, Fast Accurate Bids provides access to its data in the Design and Pricing Page. This includes the item information, the decoration selections and other settings on the Design and Pricing page, as well as the price settings in effect at the time that the line item was created. You can then make the changes you want and click **Add to Line Items List** to create a new line item.

The concept behind editing line items is that you use the data from an existing line item to create a new one and, once you're done, you can choose whether you want to delete the original line item or keep it.

This means that when editing a line item, the last step is to delete the original version of the line item. It also means that the process is very convenient for adding additional lines to a bid that are based on an existing line item. For example, suppose the following:

- You create a bid for 100 Gildan 2000 T-shirts with a 2-color design printed on the front.
- After sending the bid to your customer, he provides the following reply:
  - He now wants to add a 2-color design to the back of the shirts.
  - He also wants a cost comparison for using the Gildan shirts and American Apparel 2001.

To edit the bid, proceed as follows,

1. On the Line Items Page, click the **Open Bid** button and open the **.bid** file for the bid you sent to your customer.
   Here's what the Line Items Page will look like when the bid opens.

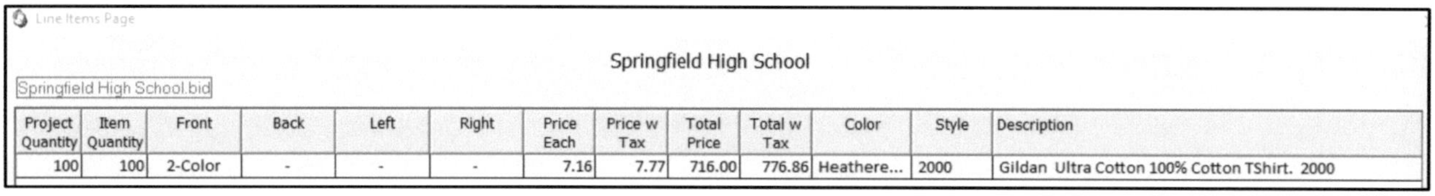

Line Items Page

Springfield High School

Springfield High School.bid

Project Quantity	Item Quantity	Front	Back	Left	Right	Price Each	Price w Tax	Total Price	Total w Tax	Color	Style	Description
100	100	2-Color	-	-	-	7.16	7.77	716.00	776.86	Heathere...	2000	Gildan Ultra Cotton 100% Cotton TShirt. 2000

   Note: When you open a saved bid, Fast Accurate Bids automatically sends the data for the first line item to the Design and Pricing Page.

2. On the Design and Pricing Page, select the check box for **Back**, add the decoration task for the 2-color print, and then click **Add to Line Items List**.

3. Open the Choose Item Page, select American Apparel as the supplier, and send a 2001 to the Design and Pricing Page, and then click **Add to Line Items List**.
   This adds the line item for the American Apparel 2001.

4. To finish the updated bid, delete the first row by right-clicking on it and selecting **Delete Row** from the menu that appears.

Here's what the Line Item Page now shows.

Line Items Page

Springfield High School

Springfield High School.bid

Project Quantity	Item Quantity	Front	Back	Left	Right	Price Each	Price w Tax	Total Price	Total w Tax	Color	Style	Description
100	100	2-Color	2-Color	-	-	9.52	10.33	952.00	1,032.92	Heathere...	2000	Gildan Ultra Cotton 100% Cotton TShirt. 2000
100	100	2-Color	2-Color	-	-	12.20	13.24	1,220.00	1,323.70	COLOR	2001	Fine Jersey S/S TShirt

You have edited the bid to add the additional information requested by the customer, you can complete the process by sending the updated bid to the customer and saving your bid file.

Things to Note:

- You can sort the line items by clicking in the header field for the column you want to sort by. Currency and numeric files sort numerically. Text fields sort alphabetically.
- You can move individual line items up or down the Line Items List as described in the section in this manual called Moving Line Items.
- Each item on the Line Items List has stored within it a record of the settings used to create it. This means that if you decide to change a profile setting while making a bid, the change you make will be used for the subsequent line items, but not for the line items you added to the Line Items Page prior to the change. For additional information on working with saved bids see Pricing Profiles and Saved Bids.
- If you click on a line item and see virtually no information in the Design and Pricing Page, it means that the line item was created using the Direct Item Feature on the Line Items Page. To make changes to these lines, click the Add Direct Item button on the Line Items page to add a new direct line item and delete the one you no longer want. For more information see Adding a direct line item.

Moving line items

You can right-click a row on the Line Items Page to move line items up or down in the line items list.

To move a line item,

1. Right-click in the row you want to move.
2. Select **Move row with the arrow keys**.
3. Use the up (or down) arrow key on your computer keyboard to move the line item.
4. Press Enter to complete the move process.

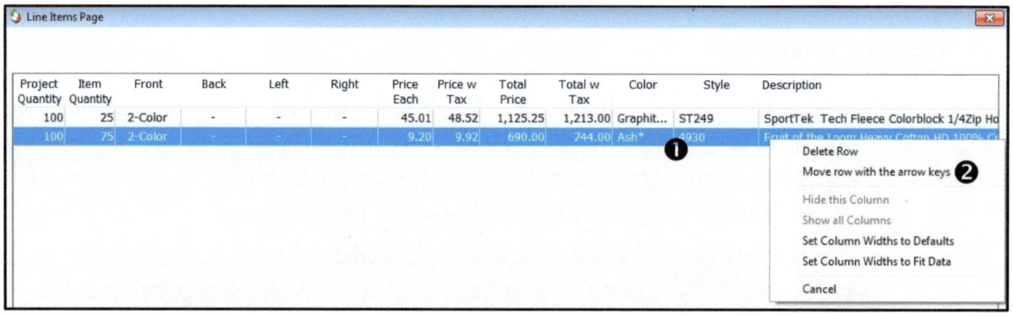

Adjusting line item column widths

You can change the column widths on the Line Items Page by dragging the dividers in the header row of the line items table. You can also right-click in the line items table to set the columns back to their default and to compact the width of the table by setting the column widths to fit the data.

To change the column widths from the header row,

1. Hover the mouse on the column border.
2. Drag to the right or left to change the width.

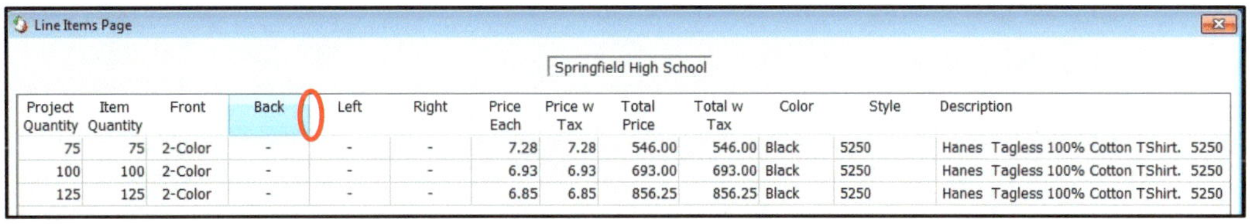

Project Quantity	Item Quantity	Front	Back	Left	Right	Price Each	Price w Tax	Total Price	Total w Tax	Color	Style	Description
75	75	2-Color	-	-	-	7.28	7.28	546.00	546.00	Black	5250	Hanes Tagless 100% Cotton TShirt. 5250
100	100	2-Color	-	-	-	6.93	6.93	693.00	693.00	Black	5250	Hanes Tagless 100% Cotton TShirt. 5250
125	125	2-Color	-	-	-	6.85	6.85	856.25	856.25	Black	5250	Hanes Tagless 100% Cotton TShirt. 5250

Things to Note:

- If you make the line item list as compact as possible, you will then be able to make it larger in the finished bid by clicking on the line item list and expanding its size.
- One of the best ways to minimize the width of the line items list is to right-click and remove the columns that are not used for bid information. For example, if the job does not call for collecting sales tax on the job, the columns for **Price w Tax** and **Total w Tax** can be removed.

Deleting line items

You can delete a line item by right-clicking in the row you want to delete.

To delete a line item,

1. Right-click in the row you want to delete.
2. Choose Delete Row.
3. Click Yes to the prompt to confirm the delete.

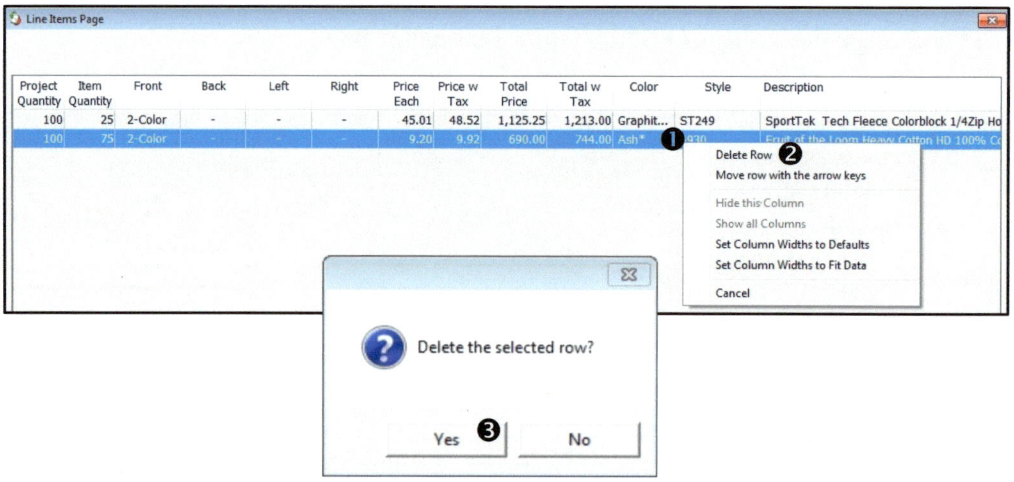

You can right-click in any line item row to delete it.

To remove a totals row, change the choice for the total to Don't Show Totals. The choices for the totals row are provided at the lower-left of the Line Items Page.

Adding a direct line item

You can add line items directly to the Line Items Page by clicking **Add Direct Item** and using the **Add Direct Item** dialog box. For example, if you prefer to list the amount for screens, artwork, or other charges as individual line items, you can do so using this feature.

To add a direct item,

1. Click **Add Direct Item**.
2. Enter the item description.
3. Enter the item quantity.
4. Enter the charge per item.
5. If taxable, select the tax check box.
6. Click Add To Line Item List.

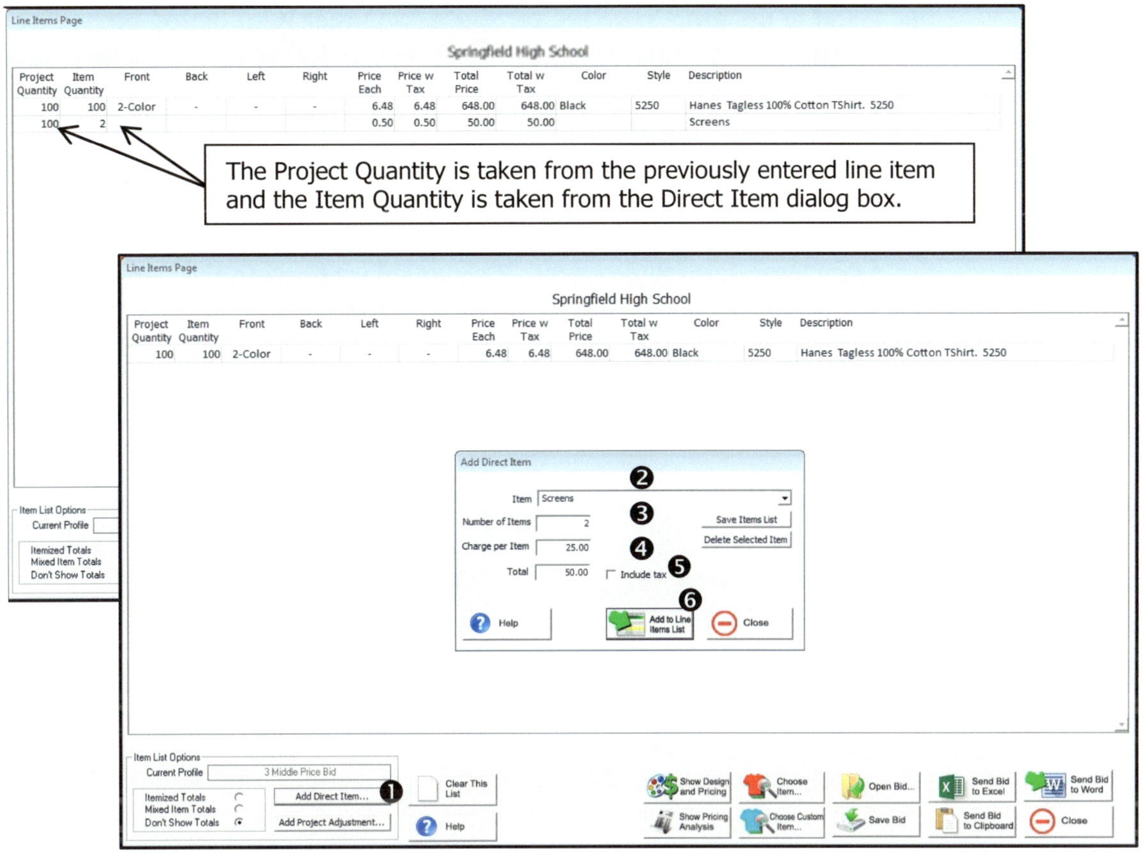

To make changes to a direct line item, open the Add Direct Line Item dialog box, create the new direct line item and delete the old one.

The difference between adding a custom item from the Design and Pricing Page and a Direct Item from the Line Items Page is that if you provide a Net Cost for a custom item, then item markup, item overhead, administrative overhead, and commission are added to custom item as specified in the associated pricing profile.

For this reason, when doing an itemized bid, the charge for preparing the screens should be added as a direct line item, with the charge for the screens set high enough to cover your administrative charges and commission. Also, you should set up a pricing profile that has the **Screen Charge/Color** set to $0.00 to avoid charging the customer twice for the cost of preparing screens. Be sure to include the word *Itemized* (or *No Screen Charge*) in the name for the profile so that it is clear that it does not include a charge for creating screens.

Things to Note

- You may add as many direct line items to bids as you want.
- For your convenience, Fast Accurate Bids provides a drop-down menu of several frequently used direct line items to select from, including one for **Send blank line.** This choice lets you add a blank line to the Line Items Page, which can be useful for creating a separation between groups of items on a bid.
- The buttons for **Delete Selected Item** and **Save Item List** let you manage the items that get saved to the dropdown list for the Add Direct Item dialog box. To add new choices to the dropdown list, enter the information in the dialog box and click **Save Item List**.
- If you delete the entry for Send blank line and then decide that you want it back, type the string **Send blank line** into the Item Description field and click the Save Item List button.
- The Price Each amount for direct items is calculated based on the **Project Quantity** on the Design and Pricing Page; not the number you enter in the field **Number of Items** in the Add Direct Item dialog box. This enables showing the correct Price Each total when you add a Mixed Items Totals row to your bid.

Adding a project adjustment

Clicking the **Add Project Adjustment** button on the Line Items Page opens a dialog box that allows you to add an additional line item that is a charge or discount to be applied to all the line items for the bid. For example, suppose your customer wants to pay for the order using an American Express Card and agrees to pay a 4% surcharge to cover the transaction fees. Adding the surcharge as a project adjustment would allow the customer to clearly see the charge as an additional line item.

To add a project adjustment,

1. Click the Add Project Adjustment button.
2. Enter the amount of the adjustment and the description.
3. Enter the description for the adjustment.
4. Click Add to Line Items.
5. The adjustment is added as a line item on the bid.

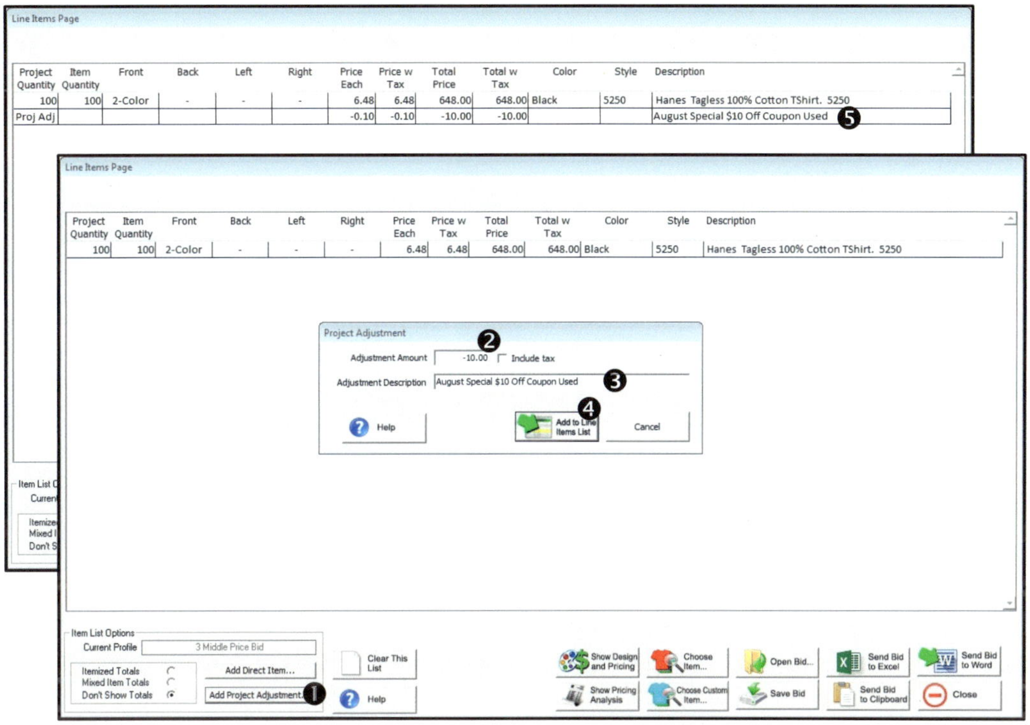

To make changes to a project adjustment, open the Add Project Adjustment dialog box, click **Yes** to the prompt to replace the current project adjustment, and create the new one.

Things to Note

- You can enter only one project adjustment per bid.
- You can enter a project adjustment as a specific amount or as a percent and as a positive or negative number. For example, to enter a percentage discount, enter a minus sign in front of the number and a percent sign after it.
- When using a percent for the project adjustment, the adjustment percentage is applied to the sum of the line items.

- To apply a price adjustment to just a single line item, use the field **Set Price Adjustment** on the Design and Pricing Page. For example when you are creating a standard bid (i.e., pricing on various quantities such as 24, 36, 48 items), it would not make sense to use a project adjustment to provide a single adjustment on the sum of all the line items.
- Fast Accurate Bids displays the line for a project adjustment as either the last line on the Line Items List, or the line just before the totals row, if you add a totals row to the list.

Adding a totals row to a bid

You have three choices for totals. These are: show no totals at all, show the total with a total price each, and show the total with no price each. By default, Fast Accurate Bids displays the line items list with no totals.

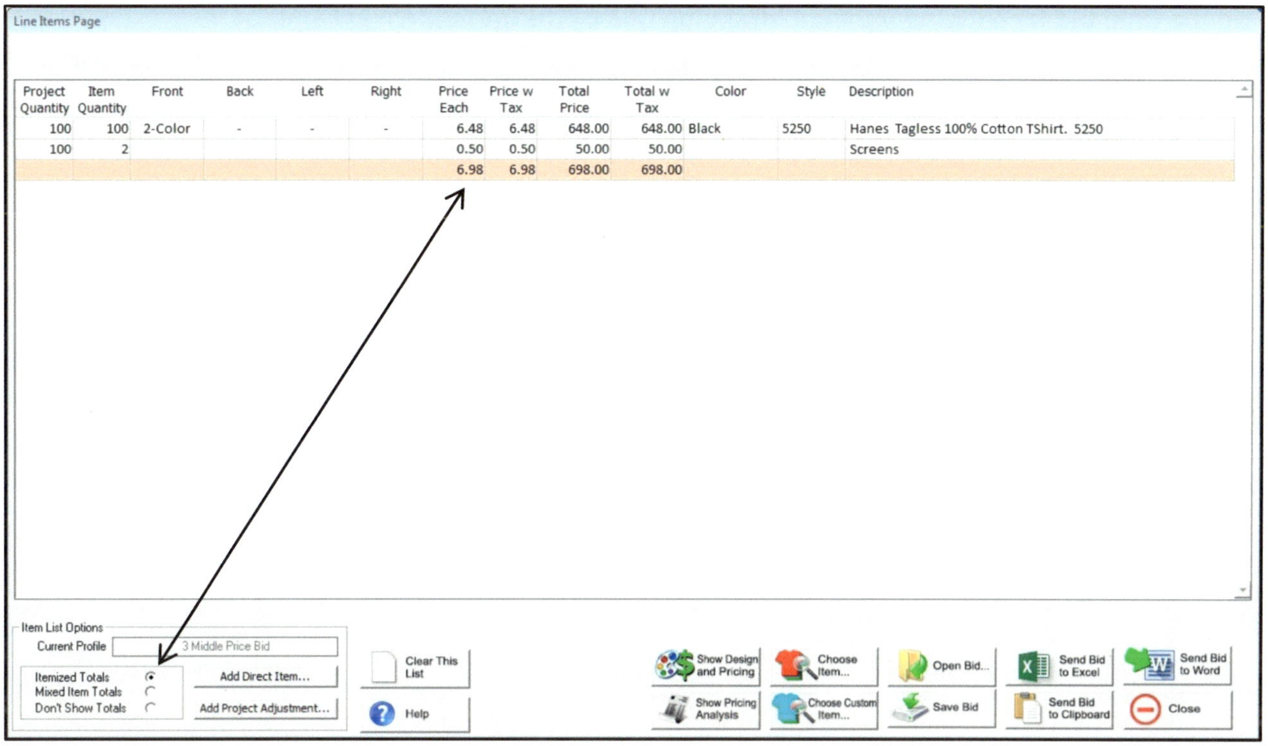

If you add a totals row and then decide that you don't want it, you can remove it by changing your choice for the totals to **Don't Show Totals**.

Hiding line items table columns

To hide any of the columns from the line items table, right-click in the header of the column you want to remove and select **Hide this column** from the menu that appears.

In the screen shot below the columns Left, Right, Each with Tax, and Total with Tax have been hidden. When you hide the columns that are not needed, you can make the line items table larger on the final bid by clicking on it and dragging one of the corners to resize it.

To redisplay the columns, right-click any place in the header row of the table and select **Show All Columns** from the menu that appears.

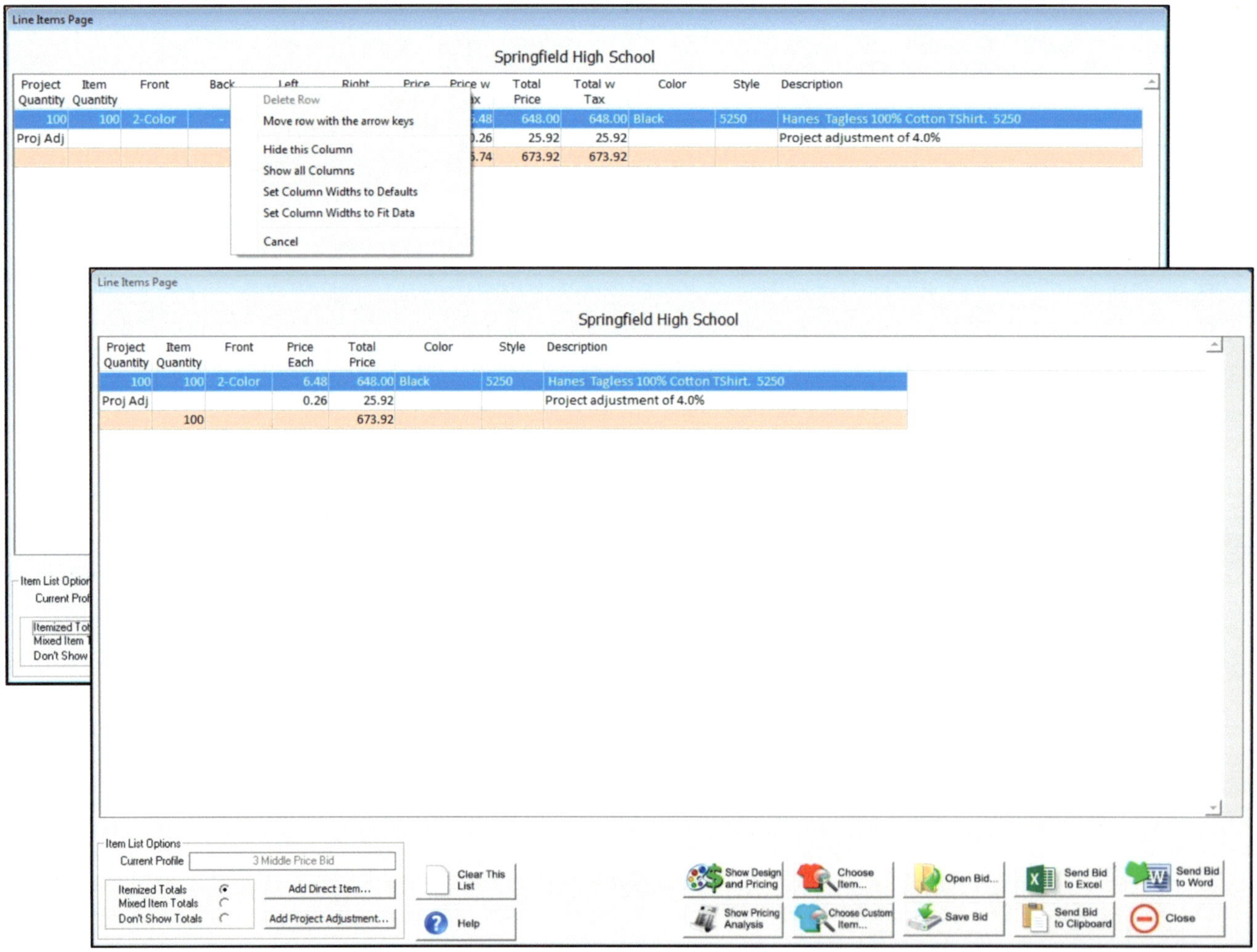

Creating the finished bid

Fast Accurate Bids lets you finish your customer bids by using either Microsoft Word or copying the line items information to the Windows clipboard and using Outlook (or whatever other means you prefer) for communicating with your customers.

The information that follows describes how to use each of these methods.

Using Microsoft Word

When you click **Send Bid to Word**, the word file opens with your boilerplate information for bids and automatically includes the date, customer name and address, and the line items table.

From this point forward, the file behaves just as any other file created in Word. There are no Fast Accurate Bids controls manipulating it. You can edit the text and save the finished bid to any location on your system that you choose. Depending on the capabilities of your Word software, you can save the file as a Word file or PDF to send to the customer, print it, or copy the text and paste it into an email.

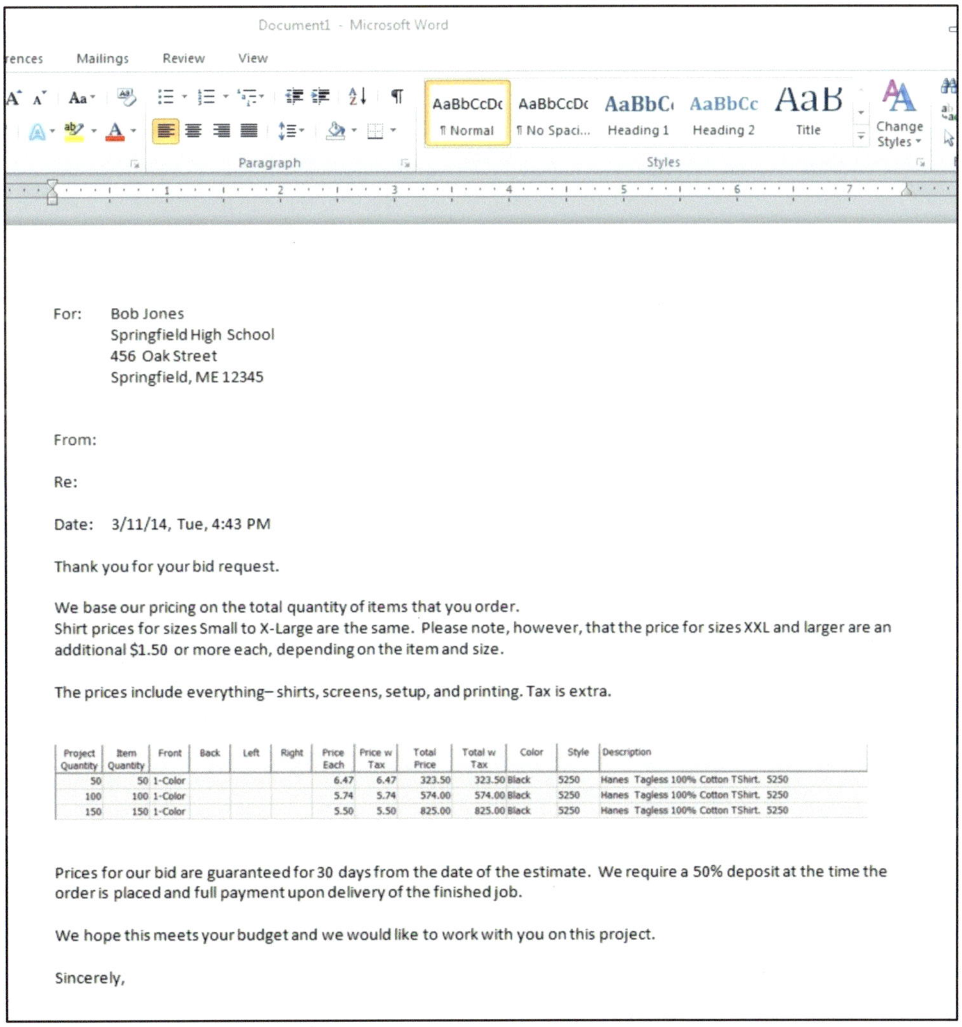

Document1 - Microsoft Word

For: Bob Jones
Springfield High School
456 Oak Street
Springfield, ME 12345

From:

Re:

Date: 3/11/14, Tue, 4:43 PM

Thank you for your bid request.

We base our pricing on the total quantity of items that you order.
Shirt prices for sizes Small to X-Large are the same. Please note, however, that the price for sizes XXL and larger are an additional $1.50 or more each, depending on the item and size.

The prices include everything– shirts, screens, setup, and printing. Tax is extra.

Project Quantity	Item Quantity	Front	Back	Left	Right	Price Each	Price w Tax	Total Price	Total w Tax	Color	Style	Description
50	50	1-Color				6.47	6.47	323.50	323.50	Black	5250	Hanes Tagless 100% Cotton TShirt. 5250
100	100	1-Color				5.74	5.74	574.00	574.00	Black	5250	Hanes Tagless 100% Cotton TShirt. 5250
150	150	1-Color				5.50	5.50	825.00	825.00	Black	5250	Hanes Tagless 100% Cotton TShirt. 5250

Prices for our bid are guaranteed for 30 days from the date of the estimate. We require a 50% deposit at the time the order is placed and full payment upon delivery of the finished job.

We hope this meets your budget and we would like to work with you on this project.

Sincerely,

Tip: You can make the line items list larger by removing the unused fields before sending the bid to Word.

For example, in this bid, the fields Back, Left, Right, Price w Tax, and Total w Tax could be removed to make the line items list larger.

Things to note

- The line items table on the finished bid is a non-editable image. This protects you from the possibility of any changes being made to this information.
- The Fast Accurate Bids bid template is a standard Word template. The *Fast Accurate Bids Shop Owner's Manual* describes how to open the template file and customize it for your business.
- If the **Send bid to Word** button is dimmed, it means Fast Accurate Bids could not find a copy of Microsoft Word on your computer. If this is the case, you can use the **Send Bid to Clipboard** button on the Line Items Page to copy the line items table into any document that you can use the Windows Paste function with. Then, when you want to start another bid, click the Clear List button on the Line Items Page to remove the line items table for the bid that is done.
- Keep in mind that if you receive an email from a customer that has been created using a plain text editor (as opposed to an html editor); you will not be able to paste the line items table into a direct reply. The reason for this is that the Fast Accurate Bids line items table is a Windows object. This protects you from the possibility of the customer changing the data on the table. Your email program will display a message if you ever have this situation. There are three choices for working around this email limitation. You can type your line item table in the body of the reply. You can send a new email with your reply. You can save the bid and attach it as a file to your reply.

Using Send Bid to Clipboard

You can copy the line items table to the Windows clipboard by clicking the **Send Bid to Clipboard** button. The Fast Accurate Bids software provides a message box to let you know that the line items table has been copied to the clipboard.

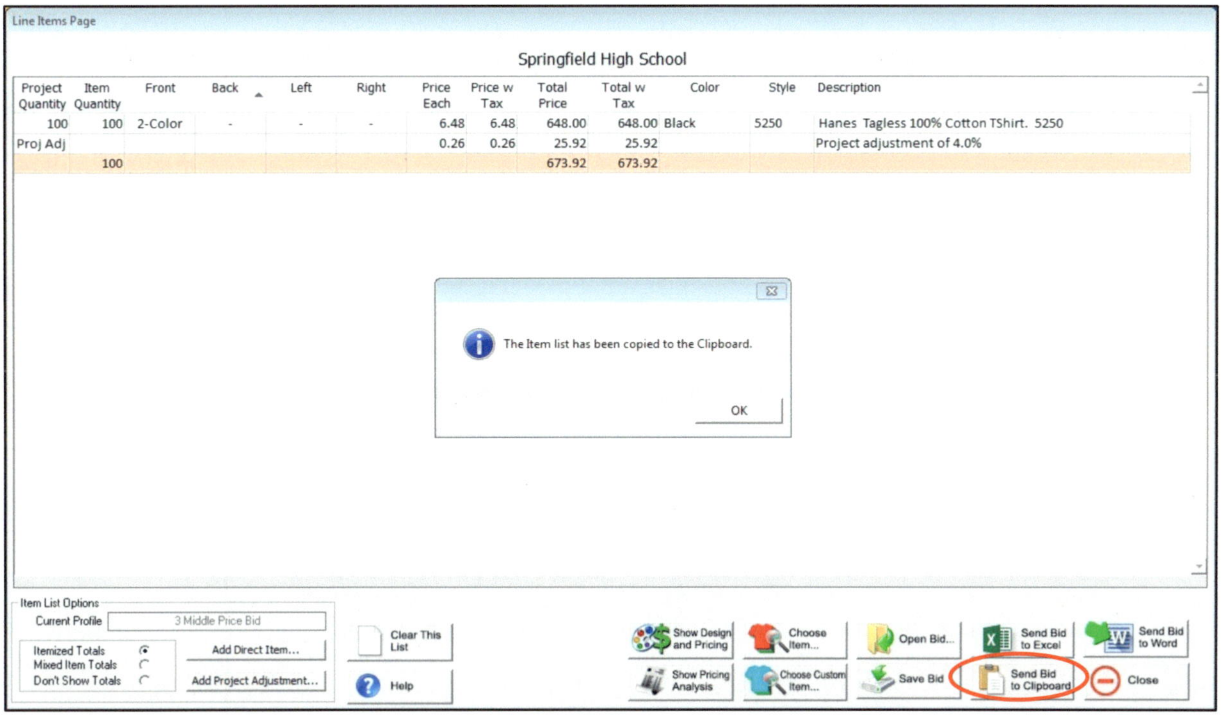

The ability to copy the line items table to the Windows clipboard can be useful for incorporating the bid information into an email.

The ability to copy and paste a line items table can also be used in combination with the Fast Accurate Bids Word file. For example, suppose you have a bid for a little league team that is for 20 embroidered hats, 20 screen printed team member T-shirts, and 100 screen printed T-shirts to sell to the fans and supporters. Instead of putting all the line items on a single table, you can set up a bid that looks like the one that follows by sending the first line item to the Word file and then copying the next two line items to the clipboard and pasting them into Word and adding the additional text by editing the Word file.

BELLINGHAM SCREEN PRINTING

For: Springfield Little League

From: Bellingham Screen Printing

Re: Caps and Shirts for baseball team

Date: 3/16/14, Sun

Here's our bid on 20 caps, 20 team shirts, and 100 additional shirts for your little league team.

We base our pricing on the total quantity of items that you order.
Shirt prices for sizes Small to X-Large are the same. Please note, however, that the price for sizes XXL and larger are an additional $1.50 or more each, depending on the item and size.

The prices include everything– shirts, screens, setup, and printing. Tax is extra.

20 Navy Caps, embroidered in white on the front

Project Quantity	Item Quantity	Front	Back	Left	Right	Price Each	Price w Tax	Total Price	Total w Tax	Color	Style	Description
20	20	Emb				18.14	18.14	362.80	362.80	Navy	C865	Port Authority Flexfit Cap. C865

20 Navy and White Shirts for players - screen printed - white on front, players' name and number on the back

Project Quantity	Item Quantity	Front	Back	Left	Right	Price Each	Price w Tax	Total Price	Total w Tax	Color	Style	Description
20	20	1-Color				12.83	12.83	256.60	256.60	White/Navy	YT200	SportTek Youth Colorblock Raglan Jersey. YT200

100 Navy Shirts for fans and supporters, screen printed – white on front

Project Quantity	Item Quantity	Front	Back	Left	Right	Price Each	Price w Tax	Total Price	Total w Tax	Color	Style	Description
100	100	1-Color				6.05	6.58	605.00	658.00	Navy	5250	Hanes Tagless 100% Cotton TShirt. 5250

Prices for our bid are guaranteed for 30 days from the date of the estimate. We require a 50% deposit at the time the order is placed and full payment upon delivery of the finished job.

We hope this meets your budget and we would like to work with you on this project.

Sincerely,

Steve Steiger, Owner
Bellingham Screen Printing
4410 Northwest Drive
Bellingham, WA 98225
360-920-0114

Note: Bellingham Screen Printing is our sister company.

Using Send Bid to Microsoft Excel

The Send Bid to Excel Button on the Line Items Page lets you save the line items list as a Microsoft Excel spreadsheet.

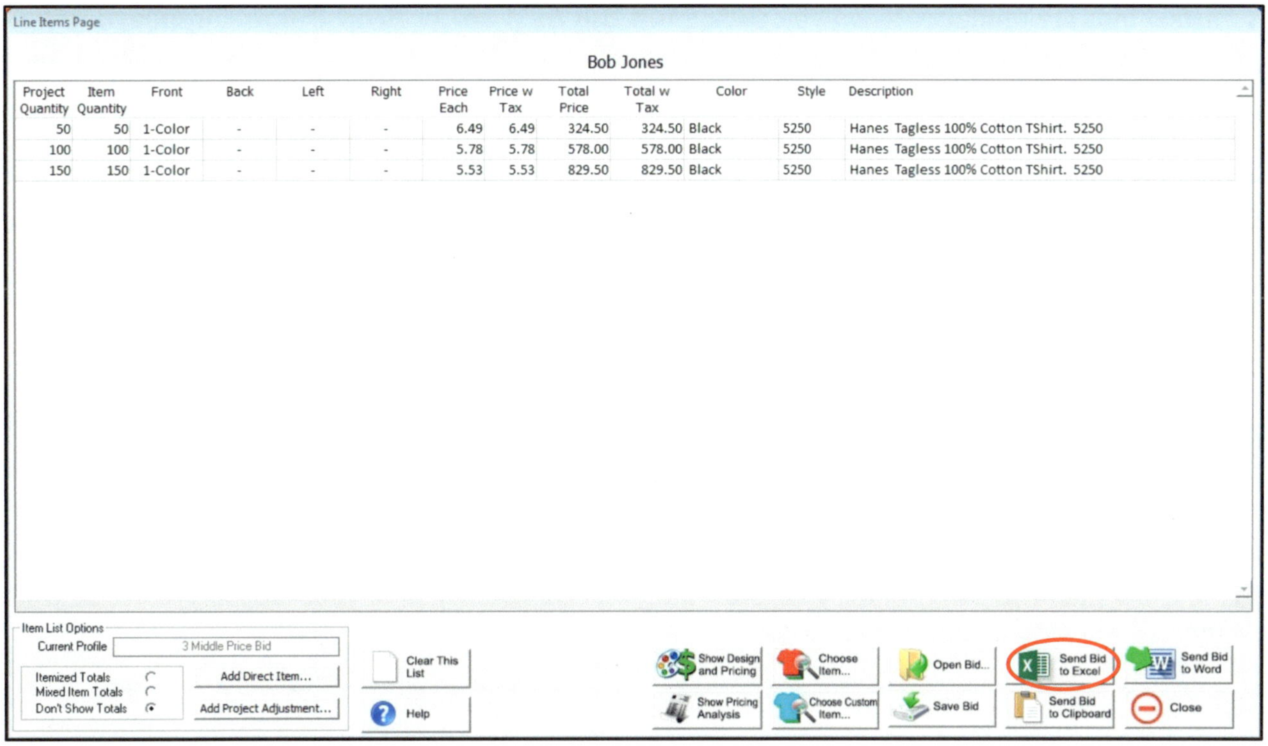

The information you enter in the **Prepared For** field on the Design and Pricing Page is used to automatically create a title for the spreadsheet.

	A	B	C	D	E	F	G	H	I	J	K	L	M
1	**Bob Jones**												
2													
3	**Project Quantity**	**Item Quantity**	**Front**	**Back**	**Left**	**Right**	**Price Each**	**Price w Tax**	**Total Price**	**Total w Tax**	**Color**	**Style**	**Description**
4	50	50	1-Color	-	-	-	6.49	6.49	324.5	324.5	Black	5250	Hanes Tagless 100% Cotton TShirt. 5250
5	100	100	1-Color	-	-	-	5.78	5.78	578	578	Black	5250	Hanes Tagless 100% Cotton TShirt. 5250
6	150	150	1-Color	-	-	-	5.53	5.53	829.5	829.5	Black	5250	Hanes Tagless 100% Cotton TShirt. 5250

This feature can be useful for doing such things as copying line item information for pasting into QuickBooks for creating customer invoices and anything else you want to use it for.

For information on price lists, see the Fast Accurate Bids Shop Owner's Manual.

Saving and restoring bids

When using Fast Accurate Bids, it's important to understand the difference between finished bids and bid files.

Finished bids are produced when you click **Send Bid to Word** or **Send Bid to Clipboard** to finish a bid**.** This is the information that you send to your customer whether it's via a Word file, email, or whatever other means you use to provide information to your customer.

Bid files are produced when you click **Save Bid** to save the current bid information to your Windows file system. Bid files always end with the file extension **.bid**.

Saving bid files

The **Save Bid** button on the Line Items Page lets you save your bids at any time. To retrieve your saved bids, there is an **Open Bid** button on both the Line Items Page and the Design and Pricing Page.

When you use the save bid feature for the first time, Fast Accurate Bids provides the default location **My Documents/Fast Accurate Bids/Bid File.** (The **My Documents** directory is the same directory as **Library | Documents,** whichever computer file path you are accustomed to using will bring you to the same files.)

This is the intended location for your bids, but you can actually save your bids anywhere in your Windows file system that you choose.

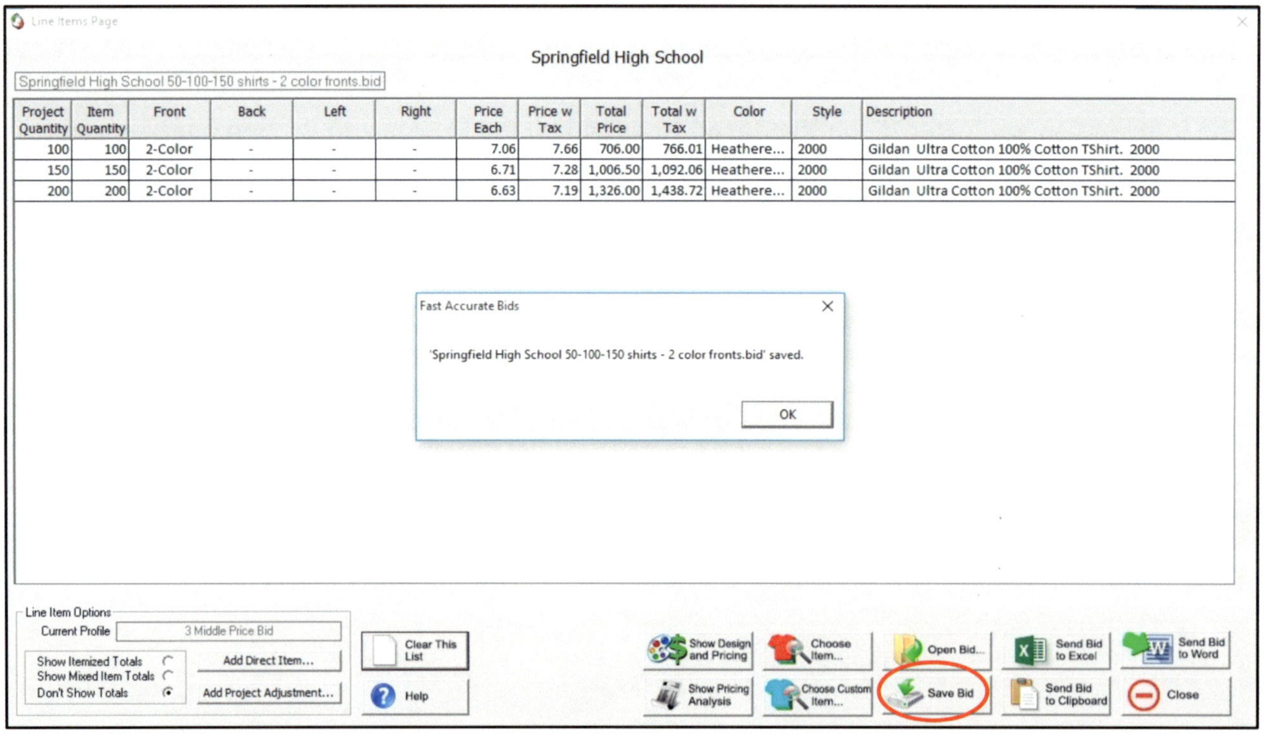

Fast Accurate Bids remembers the location of your last saved bid and automatically navigates to that location the next time you click the **Save Bid** or **Open Bid** buttons.

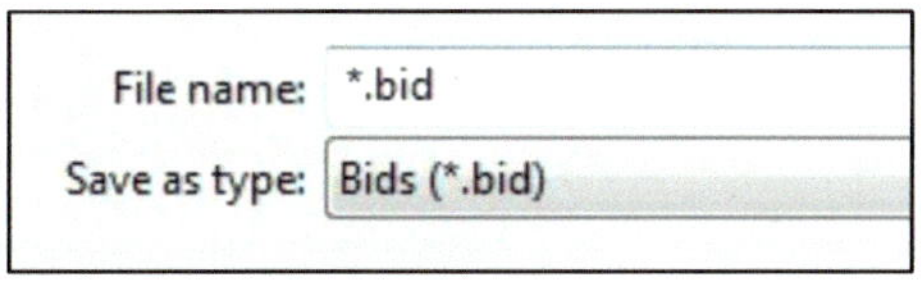

Every time that you save a bid, (regardless of whether it's a brand new bid you are creating for the first time, or a saved bid that you have just updated), the file name for saving the file defaults to ***.bid** so that you don't inadvertently overwrite an earlier version of a bid file that you want to keep on your system.

In instances when you want to save your work to the same file name (e.g., when you start a bid, save your partially finished work, and later come back later to complete it), just click on that file name in the Save Bid window to select it as the file name to write your work to. This will replace *.bid with the fine name you selected.

Tip: To assist you in organizing your bids, consider using a naming convention that is composed of the customer's name, business name, number and color of the items, and decoration. For example, **Bob Jones-Springfield High School-100 Black Shirts–1 Color Front.bid**.

Opening saved bids

Fast Accurate Bids provides an **Open Bid** button on both the Design and Pricing Page and the Line Items Page. When you click this button, the Open Saved Bid dialog box appears showing the location that you used the last time you saved a bid.

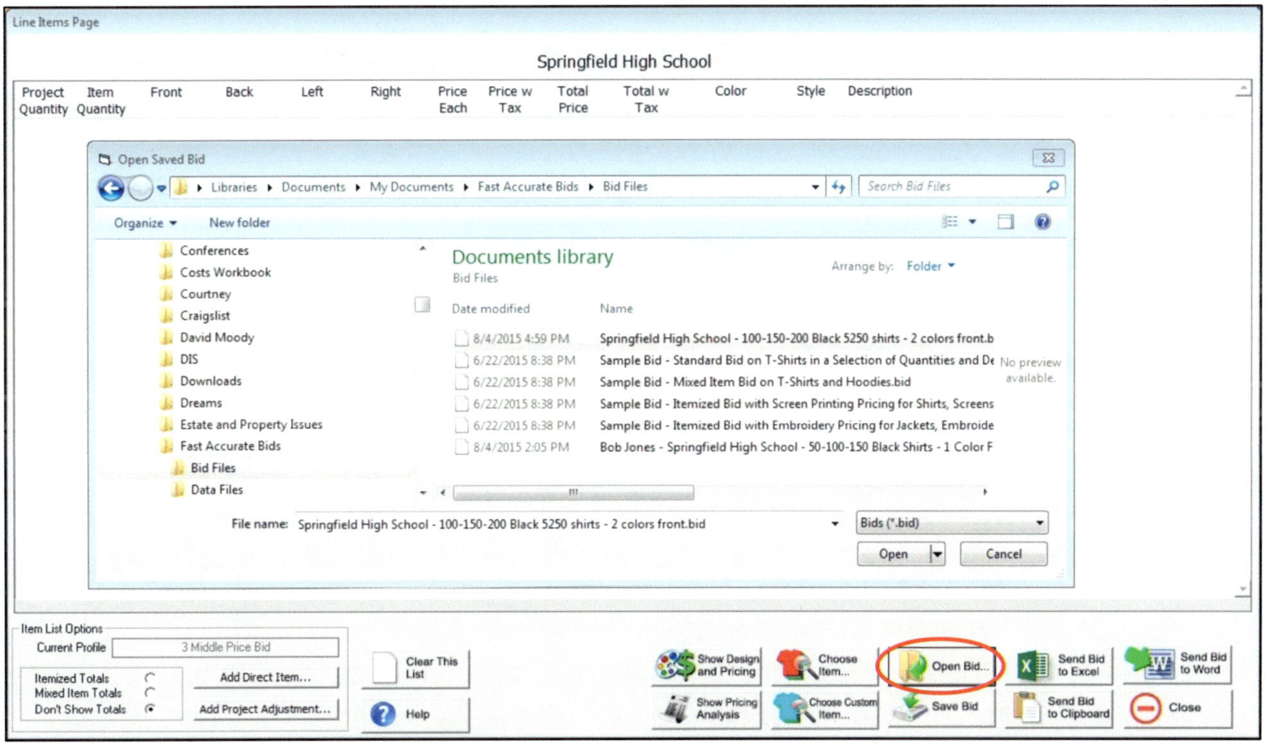

The Line Items Page displays the file name for the currently open bid at the upper-left side of the page.

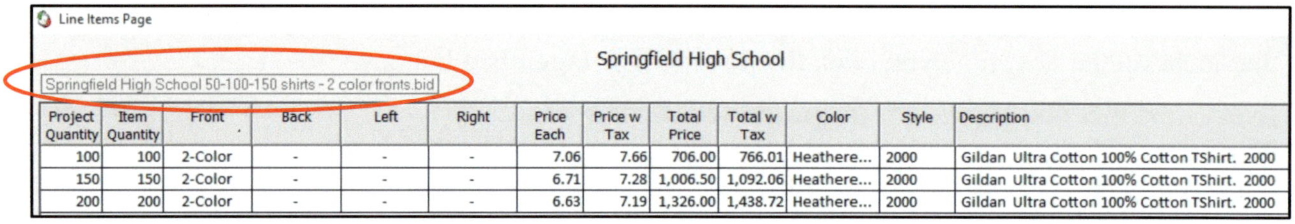

Line Items Page

Springfield High School

Springfield High School 50-100-150 shirts - 2 color fronts.bid

Project Quantity	Item Quantity	Front	Back	Left	Right	Price Each	Price w Tax	Total Price	Total w Tax	Color	Style	Description
100	100	2-Color	-	-	-	7.06	7.66	706.00	766.01	Heathere...	2000	Gildan Ultra Cotton 100% Cotton TShirt. 2000
150	150	2-Color	-	-	-	6.71	7.28	1,006.50	1,092.06	Heathere...	2000	Gildan Ultra Cotton 100% Cotton TShirt. 2000
200	200	2-Color	-	-	-	6.63	7.19	1,326.00	1,438.72	Heathere...	2000	Gildan Ultra Cotton 100% Cotton TShirt. 2000

You can share bid files with other Fast Accurate Bids users the same way that you share other types of files. For example, if you work in a company that uses a networked environment, just browse to the computer with the bid file you want to see and open it.

For computers that you are not able to access via the Open Bid dialog box, consider sending the bid file as an attachment to an email and have the person you send it to save it to their computer for opening from Fast Accurate Bids. Once the **.bid** file has been saved to the new location, then it can be opened by clicking the **Open Bid** button provided on both the Fast Accurate Bids Line Items Page and Design and Pricing Page.

Never attempt to work with bid files outside of the Fast Accurate Bids program and keep in mind that it would be pointless to send a bid file to someone who does not have a copy of Fast Accurate Bids with which to open it.

Pricing Profiles and Saved Bids

Fast Accurate Bids saves the pricing profile information in the bid files on a line-item-by-line-item basis. This means that when you click **Open Bid** to work with a bid you previously created (or one created by another user), you can be assured that the pricing information is the same as it was when the bid was originally created.

In most cases, you will probably be working with bids that you have created and the pricing profiles you used to create the bid will be a match to the pricing profiles on your computer.

When pricing profile settings are different

In instances where the settings associated with a line item on a saved bid are different than settings for the current version of the same pricing profile, a message is displayed on the Line Items Page at the top of the line items list. This message is always related to the currently selected line item and indicates whether the last-saved date for the pricing profile associated with the line item is older or newer than your current pricing profile.

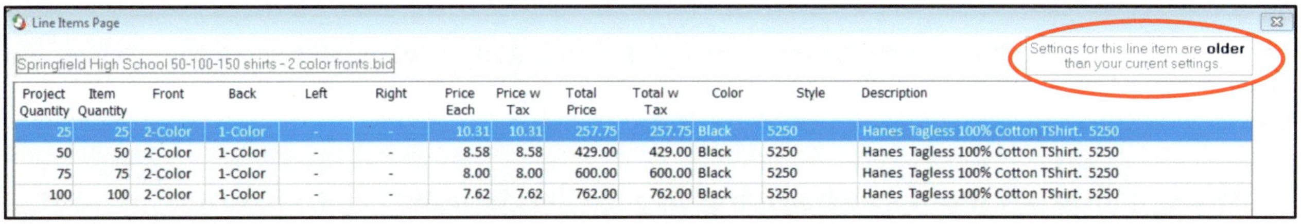

Examples for working with differing pricing profiles

The information that follows provides examples to help you understand how to work with bids for which there are differing settings for profiles that use the same name.

Working with a bid that uses an older pricing profile and you want to keep the older price settings

Suppose that you open a bid you made a month ago, you have since changed one or more of your pricing profile settings, but you want to keep your earlier pricing for the bid.

In this instance, you can edit the bid in the same way that you would edit a bid with no changes to the pricing profile. In other words, for each line item that you want to edit,

1. Click the line item to send its data to the Design and Pricing Page.
2. Make the changes you want to the line item.
3. Send the updated line item to the Line Items Page.
4. Right-click and delete the original line item you no longer want.

The reason for this is that Fast Accurate Bids takes the pricing information for a saved bid from the line items that you click on in the Line Items Page.

Working with a bid that uses a newer pricing profile and you want to update the bid to your current pricing

Suppose that you open a bid from a year ago for a customer who places an identical order every year for shirts for his summer camp. You've updated your pricing profiles in the past year and you want to use your current pricing for this year's bid.

Update the bid as follows,

1. Click on the first line item on the bid to send its data to the Design and Pricing page. ***Note:*** This sends the line item's data to both the Design and Pricing Page and the Profile Settings Page.
2. On the Design and Pricing Page, open the **Choose Profile** drop-down list and select the pricing profile of the same name from the list. This changes the pricing to the settings used in the current pricing profile on your computer.
3. Click **Send to Line Items Page** to send the updated version of the line item to the Line Items Page.
4. Right-click on the original version of the line item and delete it.
5. Repeat steps 1 through 4 for each of the line items on the bid.
6. When you're done editing the bid, click **Save Bid** to save the bid.

Note: Depending on the number of line items on the bid, it may be quicker and easier to just create a new bid based on the old one instead of editing each of the line items.

Working with a bid that uses a pricing profile that is newer than the one on your computer and you want to update your computer to use the newer profile settings

Suppose that your sales manager sends you a bid file and asks you to update the pricing profiles on your computer using the line items in the bid.

Update your pricing profiles as follows:

1. Open the bid from Fast Accurate Bids.
   Note: This automatically sends data for the first line item to both the Design and Pricing Page and the Profile Settings Page.
2. If you see a message that the profile settings for the line item are newer than your current settings, then go to the Design and Pricing Page and click **Show Settings**.
   Note: If you don't see this message, you can skip step 3 and go to the next line item since there are no differences between the settings for the line item and the pricing profile on your computer.

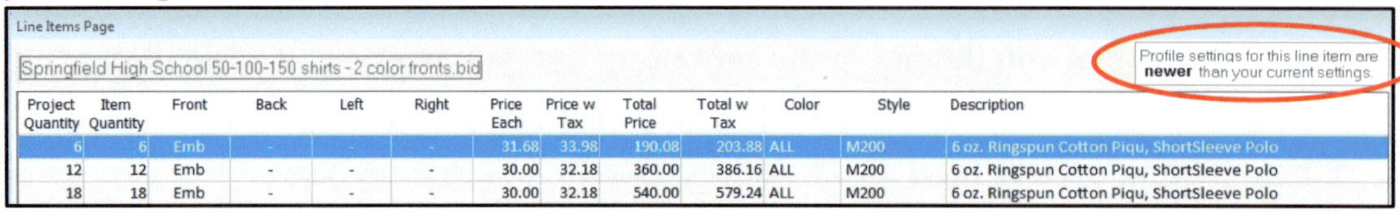

3. In the Setting Page that appears, click **Save Current Profile**.
   Note: This overwrites the pricing profile settings on your computer with the ones from the line item.
4. Click in each subsequent line item on the bid to see if there are additional pricing profiles that need updating. If so, repeat steps 2 and 3.
5. Once you've checked all the line items, **Clear this List** and **No** to the prompt to save the bid.
   Note: You don't need to save the bid because you are not updating it. You are only updating the profile settings on your computer.

Working with a bid that uses a pricing profile you do not have on your computer

When you open a bid that uses a pricing profile that does not exist on your computer, Fast Accurate Bids adds the pricing profile to your computer temporarily so that it's available for editing the bid. You can use the pricing profile in the same way that you would use any other of your Fast Accurate Bids for Embroidery pricing profiles.

If you want to keep the temporary pricing profile around after editing the bid, open the Profile Settings Page, and click the **Save Current Profile** button; otherwise, it is removed from your computer when you close out of the bid that uses it.

Glossary

Admin Overhead - is a field in the Overhead Charges area of the Profile Settings Page. This field sets the percentage to be charged to cover overhead costs such as your production margin, rent, non-billable staff time, equipment costs, utility bills, and insurance. When used, administrative overhead is calculated on the price of the item just prior to applying the commission percentage. (Admin Overhead is not applied on the net cost for items.)

Bid Files - are produced when you click **Save Bid** on the Line Items Page to save the current bid information to your Windows file system. Bid files always end with the file extension **.bid**.

Calculated Shipping - is the estimated cost of shipping the items from your supplier to your shop. It is calculated as the higher of either (Net Item Price x Items per Style x Wholesale Shipping Percent) or the amount specified on the Setting Page in the field Wholesale Min Shipping.

Check In/Layout - is a field in the Overhead Charges area of the Profile Settings Page. This field sets the charge per item that you want used to cover the time it takes to unpack items, count them, stack them for decoration, lay them out again after decoration, recount them, and repack them for delivery.

Custom Ink Charge/Color - is a field in the Screen Printing Charges area of the Profile Settings Page. This field sets the additional amount for screen printing on items that require an additive for the ink. This charge is intended to recover the cost of ink that must be discarded after printing the job, for example printing on nylon items. The custom ink charge per color is multiplied by the sum of the **Screen Print** quantities and the **Item Qty** to determine the amount to charge.

Custom Item - is any item that you cannot select from the Choose Item Page because you do not have a supplier connector for the company from which you intend to order them. The Custom Item Page lets you set up and manage your list of custom items.

DTG - is also known as digital direct to garment printing, D2G printing, digital garment printing and inkjet to garment printing. It is a process of printing on textiles and garments using specialized or modified inkjet technology. DTG printers use specialty inks (inkjet textile inks) that are applied to the textile directly and are absorbed by the fibers.

Discharge Printing - is a method of applying a design to dyed cotton fabric by printing a color-removing agent, such as chlorine or hydrosulfite, to bleach out a white or light pattern on the darker colored ground. In color-discharge printing, a dye impervious to the bleaching agent is combined with it, producing a colored design instead of white.

Exclude Overhead Charges - is a check box that appears in the Name/Number Charges, Embroidery Charges, and Other Decoration Charges areas of the Profile Settings Page. These check boxes let you to specify whether you want the associated charges to be the exact amount to the customer or whether you want Fast Accurate Bids to calculate and add Check In/Layout, Admin Overhead, and Commission to these charges. Thus, if you have already factored in your handling, overhead, and commission on your embroidery other decoration and name and number charges, then selecting this check box lets you continue to use the amount for these charges that you are accustomed to using.

Flashing Charge/Color - is a field in the Screen Printing Charges area of the Profile Settings Page. This field sets the additional amount you charge to cover the time it takes to flash cure ink during printing. There are fields on the Design and Pricing Page for selecting the number of flashes for each of the sides of the item.

Ink Surcharge for Flashing - is a field in the Screen Printing Charges area of the Profile Settings Page. This field sets the markup percentage that is applied to the **Ink Charge/Color** field to calculate the ink charge for items that are flashed.

Flashing - is the process of using a heating unit on a screen printed garment while it is still on the press. The temperature of the ink layer on the garment is raised to the point where the ink begins to dry but is not completely cured. The ink will be dry to the touch and will form a solid surface on which to print additional colors. When the garment is run through the dryer the flashed layer will cure completely and bond to the ink layers on top.

Full Search - is one of the two options on the Update Prices dialog box. A Full Search enables the Fast Accurate Bids Supplier Connector to search your computer's full hard drive to locate the downloaded supplier pricing file. If you prefer to specify a directory for downloading the supplier pricing files that is other than the Windows Downloads directory, use this search option.

Ink Color Change - is a field in the Screen Printing area of the Design and Pricing Page. This field lets you add a charge if the job requires changing the ink color for one or more screens. This charge is intended to cover the time it takes to clean the ink from a screen and re-ink it. The amount that gets charged is determined by the amount in the field **Ink Color Change** on the Profile Settings Page.

Ink Charge/Color - is a field in the Screen Printing Charges area of the Profile Settings Page. This field sets the amount for ink to print one color on one item.

Item Cost - is a field on the Design and Pricing page. This is the amount that you pay to your supplier for the items you sell. When you enter an item by selecting it from the Choose Item Page, the item cost is taken from the data in the supplier's pricing file. When you enter an item using the Custom Item Page, the item cost in the **Item Cost** field is taken from the data from that page.

Item Overhead - is a field in the Item Charges area of the Profile Settings Page. This field sets the percentage to be charged to cover costs such as misprints, defective items, time for ordering items, etc. When used, item overhead is applied to the item cost of the items sold.

Item Qty - is a field on the Design and Pricing page that lets you enter the quantity for a particular line item. See also Project Qty.

Item Qty Markups – is a table on the Profile Settings Page. This table defines the markup on the

Itemized Bids - show the pricing for each of the components of an apparel decoration job as opposed to standard bids and mixed item bids which show inclusive pricing. For example, an itemized bid for embroidery might show the price for the undecorated garment, the digitizing, and the embroidery. Itemized bids often show both a total price per item and total price for the job.

Mixed Item Bid – is a bid that presents an assortment of items that will receive the same decoration. For example, a mixed item bid might offer the pricing for placing the same image on 100 T-Shirts, 25 sweatshirts, and 25 hoodies. Mixed item bids show the price per item and can optionally have a totals row as well to show the total number of items and the total price for the job.

Name - is a field in the Name/Number Charges area of the Profile Settings Page. This field sets the amount you charge for putting individual names (or any individual words) on shirts. For example, putting individual employees' names and their job titles on shirts. The charge for Name gets applied when you select the check box for **Individual Name** on the Design and Pricing Page.

Owner Mode- when you set up a password in Fast Accurate Bids, you are actually setting the ability for the software to run in either Owner mode or User mode. Owner mode means that the Choose Item, Design and Pricing, and Line Items pages provide buttons to access the Profile Settings Page and the Pricing Analysis Page. The program can be started in Owner mode by entering the correct password in the field **Enter Password** on the Design and Pricing Page. If no password is set, the program operates in the same manner as it does in Owner mode.

Price List Creator - is a separately purchasable extension for Fast Accurate Bids that lets you use the Fast Accurate Bids calculation engine to easily and quickly create price lists.

Pricing Profile - is a list of the charges, markups, discounts, and other settings that are used as the variable values for this program that has been saved under a descriptive name so that you can select it for use when creating bids. This information includes all the settings and values on the Fast Accurate Bids Profile Settings Page and the name in the Prepared By field on the Design and Pricing Page. Pricing profiles end with the file suffix **.pro**.

Printing Charge/Color - is a field in the Screen Printing Charges area of the Profile Settings Page. This field sets the amount for labor to print one color on one item.

Project Qty - is the total of all items for the bid if customer wants the same decoration on different types of items. See also Item Qty.

Quick Search - is one of the two options on the Update Prices dialog box. A Quick Search limits searching for a downloaded supplier pricing file to just your Windows downloads folder. This option can be used to significantly speed up the process for updating the supplier prices if you allow the pricing file to be downloaded to your Windows Downloads folder.

Screen Charge/Color - is a field in the Screen Printing Charges area of the Profile Settings Page. This field is the cost for each screen for printing. This is intended to cover the labor and materials associated with the use of the screen.

The labor portion consists of the cost of coating the screen, burning the image on it, taping it for printing, registering it on the press, and after the job is done, reclaiming it for future work.

The materials portion consists of a percentage of the cost screen itself (which is based on the number of times the screen can be used), the emulsion for the screen, the film for the image, the tape, and the chemicals.

Standard Bids - present an assortment of choices so the customer can choose one. For example, a standard bid might offer a choice of quantities (24, 36, 48), or a choice of garments (for example, good, better, best) to allow the customer to select the one that is the best match for what he wants. Standard bids show the price per item and don't provide a totals row since the underlying assumption is that the customer will only select one of the options offered by the bid.

Supplier Connector - is the generic name for the programs Fast Accurate Bids provides for downloading and working with the electronic supplier pricing files available from wholesale apparel companies. Fast Accurate Bids comes with supplier connectors for SanMar, alphabroder, and American Apparel. You may also purchase additional supplier connectors at that time or later whenever you want.

User Mode - when you set up a password in Fast Accurate Bids, you are actually setting the ability for the software to run in either Owner mode or User mode. User mode means that the **Show Settings** and **Pricing Analysis** buttons will not appear on the Design and Pricing, Choose Item, and Line Items pages. This means that unless the user is aware of using the program in Owner mode, he or she will not even know that these pages exist.

Index

I

L

M

N

O

P

Q

R

S

T

U

W

X

Made in United States
Cleveland, OH
05 November 2026

47647249R00043